Forced Migrants and Host Societies in Egypt and Sudan

CAIRO PAPERS IN SOCIAL SCIENCE
Volume 26, Number 4, Winter 2003

Forced Migrants and Host Societies in Egypt and Sudan

by
Fabienne Le Houérou

The American University in Cairo Press
Cairo   New York

Copyright © 2006 by the American University in Cairo Press
113, Sharia Kasr el Aini, Cairo, Egypt
420 Fifth Avenue, New York, NY 10018
www.aucpress.com

All rights reserved. No part of this publication may be reproduced, stored in a retrieval system, or transmitted in any form or by any means, electronic, mechanical, photocopying, recording or otherwise, without prior written permission of the copyright owner.

Dar el Kutub No. 11369/05
ISBN 977 424 964 X

Printed in Egypt

Contents

Acknowledgments	1
Chapter 1: Introduction	3
Chapter 2: Methodology	8
Interactionism	10
Ethnomethodology	11
Toward an Anthropology of Suffering	13
Chapter 3: Cultural Aspects of the Transient Ethiopian Diaspora in Cairo	17
Movement under the Shadow of Fear	19
To be Scared in the City, to be Scared of the City	23
Chapter 4: Painful Interactions between Humanitarian Actors and Their Clients	30
Heroes and Refugees	31
Total Trust Leads to Total Disaster	33
Those Who Cannot Return: Homeless and Hopeless in Sudan	37
Chapter 5: Exile and Loss of History within the Ethiopian Diaspora in Sudan	42
Methodology	44
Presentation of Ethiopian Diaspora in Khartoum	48
Studies about Urban Refugees in Khartoum	50
Reasons for Coming to Khartoum	50

Habasha and the Representation of Time	51
The Calendar and Representations of Time	53
History and Kings in Highlanders' Traditions	53
Battlefields and Historical Memory	54
Maintaining Memory in the Midst of a Loss of History	54
Memory of Adwa	55

Chapter 6: Violence or Avoidance Strategies in Arba'a wa-Nus   60
Violence or Avoidance Strategies in Arba'a wa-Nus   60
Street Violence in Arba'a wa-Nus   62
Forced Migrants from Upper Egypt   64
Dinka Displacement in Arba'a wa-Nus   67
Giving and Giving Back   69

Chapter 7: Ordinary Contacts between Refugees from Darfur and Egyptian Society   72
Scene One   72
Analyzing the Context   74
Scene Two   78
The Context   79
Violence Committed against the Refugees   80

Chapter 8: Conclusion   85

References   90

About the Author   94

Acknowledgments

THIS RESEARCH ON THE multiplicity of relations between forced migrants and their host societies in Egypt and the Sudan has benefited from the help, ideas, and guidance of many colleagues in several countries.

My warmest gratitude goes to the immense support of Barbara Harrell-Bond and the Forced Migration and Refugee Studies program at the American University in Cairo. My thanks also go to Hussein Abdallah Guidare who was an excellent Arabic professor and translator, and to Abdel-Soukour al-Khamis for his gentleness and tremendous help and inspiration. I would like to thank Shari Saunders, who guided and corrected my very poor English, for her priceless effort, and Sari Hanafi for his uncountable encouragements and the fruitful collaborations over the years. Special thanks to my friends and colleagues in Khartoum: Bushra al-Alamin, in particular, for his rich views and his generosity in sharing with me his invaluable knowledge in the field of Refugee Studies. At the University of Khartoum, I am grateful to the head of the Development Studies and Research Centre, Mustapha Zakaria, for his precious advice and his gentle welcoming.

I was fortunate to have Dr. Nicholas Hopkins as an editor for the tremendous improvement of the manuscript and to benefit from the valuable advice of Dr. Iman Hamdy. Their sage counsel was not always followed and I am the only one responsible for the remaining mistakes or weaknesses. Most of all I would like to thank the refugees I have met during these years who have trusted me and convinced me that this field was worth defending as an intellectual challenge in the academic world.

East Africa

Chapter 1
Introduction

THE PRESENT MONOGRAPH IS a study inspired by several research projects on the theme of forced migration in Egypt and Sudan. We observed different communities in exile from East Africa in urban settings or camps: Ethiopians, Eritrean, and Sudanese in Cairo, Khartoum or in the Kassala region. Our research program started in 2000 and was completed by 2004.

The polymorphology of the results presented here is therefore the mirror of the various populations we chose to study. The common point of these communities is that they all come from one of the poorest places in Africa: the Horn at the extreme East of the continent is one of the driest regions, where competition for water can be extremely violent. Conflict and famine have succeeded each other for centuries, giving the populations a very high vulnerability that can produce a pattern of "forced migration." Chronically it was urgent for the populations at risk to escape droughts and wars; and therefore the migratory refugee phenomenon is far from being new. Moving from place to place is an ancient process in the Horn of Africa.

Meanwhile the international community adopted the juridical concept of refugee in 1951 after World War II. The new international aim was to repair what the Nazis had done to the world when they eliminated millions of people. Jurists were willing to give to the international community the tools to prevent other tyrannies through an architecture of humanly inspired international conventions. The Geneva Convention was the fruit of different efforts, and so it resembled the genocide convention and the laws concerning crimes against humanity. We have to go back to this recent past to understand the essence of the emergence of a new conscience and the genesis of the concept "refugee."

Chapter Two is an attempt to develop a theoretical approach to forced migration through the interactive theory proposed by Erving Goffman and the ethnomethodological school of Harold Garfinkel. In this first chapter we will see how heuristic it is to have a comparative analysis of the exiled populations in order not to be imprisoned by the "community approach." Most of the studies in forced migration are characterized by a monographic view tending to analyze one community, one clan, or one ethnic group for its own sake and tending to isolate the group from the rest of the social reality in exile.

Our first effort was to reject this direction very much influenced by the early anthropologists. In the 1930s the beginning of anthropology was in need of a total approach, concentrating on the study of one ethnic group. Today with the progress of the discipline the interactionist interpretation is much more heuristic in term of understanding a community through its relations with others and recognizing the frontiers of an identity in the interactive process. The "aliens" can be situated in their everyday little realities with "the hosts" to perceive what characterizes their otherness. If we insist on the methodology it is partly because the field of forced migration lacks theories and there is an absolute need to deepen our knowledge and enlightenment in this new academic field. Most of the theoretical views proposed by Social Science have proved to fail, and in particular the social network approach. We will see how the ethnomethodological school could be a major development and enrich our conceptions.

Chapter Three will study the cultural aspects of the Ethiopian Diaspora in transit in Cairo. We will point out the main elements related to the exiled Ethiopians. The Ethiopian community numbers more or less, according to our sources, between five and ten thousand persons in Cairo. Most of the community is in Egypt illegally and has therefore developed a sense of spatial instability, stress and other disorders. Being illegal can produce social suffering that can be experienced as a situation of paralysis creating a sort of social handicap. Through many testimonies and long field research in Cairo, partly in association with the legal aid program created by Barbara Harrell-Bond at the American University in Cairo (AUC), we were in a dynamic of research which helped to observe the devastating effect of absence of rights among the Ethiopian Diaspora. The extreme fright of this population provokes different sorts of alienation and regression that we propose to analyze through an anthropology of the movement, a movement under the prism of fear. We will also attempt to index the consequences of fear in terms of sociability and relations with the host society.

In Chapter Four we will make a short voyage to the camps in Northeast Sudan. This part of the publication will outline an ethnography of humanitarian actors and their clients. We will give an interpretation of the relations between aid workers and NGOs (non-governmental organizations) with refugees in the Sudanese desert. The chapter explores the interactive process at work between the so-called "blond angels" and refugees through a theatrical presentation. The dysfunction of aid is then submitted to microobservation of daily relations between HW (humanitarian workers) and the refugees. We will see how unbalanced this relation is. Workers are seen by the refugees as total saviors, absolute givers in a divine type of relation that has proved to be very dangerous for the subjects. This is especially so when the politics of the NGOs are modified. Any shift or any move on the part of the HW is interpreted by the refugees on religious grounds, while aid remains political. This short analysis will prompt us to ask ourselves philosophical questions about the morality of aid and its ethic. How is it humanly possible for the workers to accept being seen as "angels," especially when aid can be cut at any time as a result of political transactions?

Pursuing an evaluation of aid politics in the Kassala region in North East Sudan, we will explore the paradox of humanitarian politics through the situation of the Beni Amer refugees who refused to repatriate to Eritrea. The international community was pressuring them to return to Eritrea, and using the policy of blackmail the United Nations High Commissioner for Refugees (UNHCR) contributed to the plight of the refugees by closing the water pump in a camp. The bureaucrats declared that all Eritreans were expected to return to their country because the reasons that forced them to escape were no longer valid. In fact, after Eritrean independence there was no motivation for the partisans of Eritrean sovereignty to remain in Sudan, and between 1993 and 2003 thousands of Eritreans returned to their home country. However, in the Sudanese desert we met ex-refugees who refused to go back even if aid were cut by the NGOs. These Beni Amer from Eritrea were considered as "ex-refugees" and were under pressure to go against their will.

We will keep the reader interested in Sudan problematic in Chapter Five. We will study the Ethiopian Diaspora in an urban setting. Self-settled refugees in Khartoum inhabiting the neighborhood of Deim invited us to explore the multiplicity of relations between exile, memory, and history.

Forced migrations have radically displaced families, and the resulting urban exiles have raised interesting questions concerning the conservation and construction of histories. With the disruption of the family unit, historical facts related to their roots have been placed at risk, potentially threatening the identity of these communities. Within a generation, memories will fade and a crucial repository of information related to the family heritage will be lost. This pattern is characteristic of any kind of migration, whether forced or voluntary in nature. In the case of forced displacement, the problem is more acute because being labelled a refugee or asylum seeker by aid agencies and other international institutional organs threatens to limit the forced migrant's identity to a mere juridical concept. This chapter aims to historicize the last wave of Ethiopian refugees in Sudan who came after 1991, fleeing the current Tigrinya government. These groups have been in Sudan for more than 13 years now, making it particularly interesting to question their respective relations to notions of history at large.

Chapter Six will focus on the South Sudanese Diaspora in Cairo, particularly Dinka refugees and their relations with Egyptian society as found in one of Cairo's poorest neighborhoods. This chapter is based on field research conducted in Cairo in an informal area (*mantiqa 'ashwa'iya*) called Arba'a wa-Nus, which means "four and a half" in Arabic. We emphasize the notion of proximity ("vicinity") as a pertinent analytical tool to study casual relationships between hosts and their guests. From this perspective, our project aims to throw light on everyday life and meetings, avoidance or conflict strategies of actors in their day-to-day transactions, as well as to study the networks of those transactions on a micro level in a specific location. In short, we try to explore social proximity and distance within a limited spatial sphere. Our goal was to give an interpretation of the impact of the morphologies of cities on the integration process of forced migrants into the host society.

Chapter Seven is equally based on fieldwork in Cairo among exiled communities of refugees from Darfur escaping the bloody conflict opposing "Arab nomads" and African rural communities. This field research is also the product of an interactive methodology using the tool of a video camera in the heuristic process of research. The analysis below is therefore the fruit of interaction as a special angle of filming interrelations between hosts and guests in specific neighborhoods in the urban setting. The surfaces of contact between refugees from Darfur and local Egyptians will be analyzed in the light of Erving Goffman's theatrical metaphor of *mise en scène* (or presentation of self) and will be an attempt to produce an account of a series of typologies of contacts between two societies. The refugees we interviewed were victims of atrocities committed by the Janjaweed, the Arab militia reputedly funded and supported by the Sudanese government.

Displaced in the first place to Khartoum, as internally displaced migrants from Darfur they became refugees, according to the Geneva Convention, when they reached Egypt. "Displaced" in Sudan and "refugees" in Egypt, the persons we interviewed were among the two million African farmers forced to move out of Darfur because of the crimes committed by the Janjaweed and the government. Being exiled in Cairo is a second uprooting: they are submitted to a second racial discrimination. In this context, we will be analysing new forms of racism through oral violence and ordinary interaction between those newcomers in Egypt and the host society.

This patchwork of communities in exile in urban settings or in camps are presented together for a heuristic purpose in order to stress the common destiny of these African migrants in the Arab World and to focus on the very few documented phenomena of South to South migrations and globalization from below. Treating refugee flows of course throws light on the processes of circulation of the poorest souls in the world.

Chapter 2
Methodology

THE PRESENT WORK IS based on a three-year (2001 to 2004) field research project carried out in Egypt and Sudan aimed at understanding the multiple relationships between exiles, history, and memory. The research began with a focus on Abyssinian[1] forced migrants living in Egypt and in Sudan from the 1960s until today. Later, the field was enlarged to include other East African populations (Sudanese and Somalis) in Cairo in order not to be imprisoned by a communitarian approach and to open our field to comparative analysis. The research presented here on Ethiopian and Eritrean refugees compares two urban settings (Khartoum and Cairo). This comparative approach allows us to test the hypothesis that the morphologies of cities are important for the integration of the forced migrants.

Two interrogations constituted the core problem of this research. The first one was to examine the influence of an urban structure on the process of losing history. More precisely, this study examines the dissipation or conservation of memories according to residential factors. This issue was presented at the Cairo Centre d'Études et de Documentation Économiques, Juridiques et Sociales[2] in 2001 in a workshop that I organized entitled "Migrants and Refugees in Urban Areas." Further discussion of the topic took place at the American University in Cairo in 2002 when I presented a seminar entitled "Exile and Loss of History in Sudan."

The second very important question was to analyze the multiple ways migrants interacted with their hosts; thereby making an ethnography of casual exchanges and experiences between the "outsiders" and the "hosts." How do

---

1 "Abyssinian" is used here to mean a population of mixed Ethiopians and Eritreans.
2 Known by its acronym, CEDEJ.

people meet on forced occasions (streets or buses)? How do they interact in other contexts and share experiences? In this everyday, face-to-face ethnography we emphasised a spatial approach by analyzing the complete net of interactions at particular sites, e.g. neighborhoods where migrants form important communities; thus, we focused our observations in Deim (in Sudan); Mohandessin and Dokki (Cairo) for the Ethiopians and Eritreans; Arba'a wa-Nus (Cairo) for the Sudanese, and Ard al-Liwa (Cairo) for the Somalis. Arba'a wa-Nus was the site of a particular approach where we studied Sudanese displacement in its interaction with the migrations of *sa'idis* (Upper Egyptians) to Cairo. We spent many months in Arba'a wa-Nus studying two communities: the Coptic Egyptian and the Dinka of Southern Sudan.

The first part of the research concerning Ethiopians and Eritreans was the object of a quantitative approach because the combined community is very small and scattered (there are only about 8,000 to 10,000 Ethiopians and Eritreans in Cairo), and it was possible to give a very rigorous picture of the forced migrants from the Horn of Africa by interviewing 161 people in Cairo. To analyze Sudanese displacement we used another methodology, "participant observation," which is a classical tool for anthropologists and for which no questionnaire is required. The latter factor better suited our purposes because we found that the questionnaire was viewed with suspicion. Arba'a wa-Nus is an informal zone, one of the poorest in town, and people were reluctant to cooperate with a questionnaire. For these reasons it proved inappropriate for the situation, and participant observation was more successful.

Perhaps it is interesting to give a few indications about the methodology since the current publication is a product of a "hybrid union" between different theories. It marks a real crossroads between quantitative and qualitative methods, a sort of "*bricolage*" or "do-it-yourself" notion that Lévi-Strauss theorized in relation to the fabric of anthropology[3] (Levi-Strauss, 1962). The research involved some 300 interviews, direct observations and analysis of visual documents such as films (60 hours of rushes and still pictures).

A questionnaire was distributed mainly among the Ethiopians and Eritreans living in Cairo and in Khartoum. We summarized the essence of the questionnaire using a set of graphic designs included in the text. The answers provided us with the basic indicators from the community in an attempt to construct a social profile of the Ethiopian migrants in Cairo. The conclusions drawn from the questionnaire data confirm those made by Dereck Cooper in 1992 when he described the average forced migrant from Ethiopia as a young single male seeking resettlement.

---

3 The classical passages in the "Savage Mind" brought bricolage into the social sciences.

This information oriented the second step of the research by helping to construct the hypothesis of transit cultures that are built by refugees during their passage through Cairo. Social consequences of transit are shown to be very different from one ethnic group to another and this suggested that the research must always maintain a comparative approach.

All the data gathered in a quantitative mode tend to prove that Cairo is a moment of transit in a long voyage. This first evidence re-enforced the conclusions of Cooper's research when he stated that the essence of the Ethiopian migration was its transient nature (1992). The main aspect of that migration has not changed during all these years.

Interactionism

The second step aimed to understand why the Ethiopian refugees were living in such an isolated state and why they were expressing so much suffering. They described their life in Cairo as a nightmare. Other communities in Cairo, experiencing the same legal difficulties, have richer interactions with the host society. For example, everywhere on the streets of Cairo you find Sudanese working, selling, buying, and interacting in the city. Street sellers are mainly Western Sudanese coming from the Fur tribe. Contrary to this lively image, the Ethiopian community shows all the signs of withdrawing into itself. To understand this behavior we observed the daily life interactions between the sojourners in a culture of transit and their hosts. We had great interest in the ways people met during forced occasions. Analyzing the situations when people come across each other was heuristic in the sense that many points emerged in these specific moments and places.

This approach is very much inspired by Erving Goffman's studies on ordinary social interactions. We were very much influenced by his theories of building a sociology of circumstances.[4] In the case of the forced migrations, the moments people come across each other are only the result of "occurrences" that are shaped by the circumstances. In short, we wanted to highlight the importance of context. Hosts meet their guests only on rare occasions. Thus, we observed a series of interactions that remained strictly on the level of casual interrelations: moments when it was impossible to avoid, or escape, the presence of the "Others" impossible not to face these "aliens" in buses, schools, cafés, mosques, churches, clubs, hospitals, and clinics. So we turned to all these everyday situations in which people were forced to talk, to face, and to interact with others and we sought to analyse the ways

---

4 See Goffman 1959, 1963, 1968.

people would escape (avoidance strategy), face, or confront, share something, or reject each other.

We also compared different neighborhoods, conducting our investigations in Dokki, Mohandessin, Madinat Nasser, Heliopolis and New Maadi: all places where the Ethiopian Diaspora is very much present. We completed the investigation by comparing these neighborhoods with places like Arba'a wa-Nus and Ard al-Liwa. Each space created a different form of interaction. Cultural difference is then the fruit of a "permanent invention identity" as studied by Michel Wieviorka in his recent book, *La différence* (2001).

Ethnomethodology

For this field experience we borrowed many concepts from the ethnomethodological "school." Most of the techniques are not new in anthropological literature, but the way it was theorized by Harold Garfinkel is particularly interesting for the study of forced migrations. A brief account of the main concepts provides the background. These are: analyzing evidence, being a member of the community you study, and the unique competence of the actor (Garfinkel, 1967, 1986, 2002).

The idea that the actor is the only individual who is competent to tell the story of his or her culture is another major theme that inspired the approach. For us, the only ones legitimately authorized to relate this experience are the refugees themselves. This point of view was largely developed by Barbara Harrell-Bond (1986) and Ahmed Karadawi (1999). They both considered the refugee experience as the "foundation" experience, a starting point for any issue. If this revolution in the "*point of view*" did not take place, a book like Harrell-Bond's *Imposing Aid* would never have been written. Everything in this study is constructed with the idea that the refugee is the only person who has the ability to tell us about the process of a forced migration. The value of the study lies in its ability to de-construct the concepts used by humanitarian organizations and to break the "monopoly" that these organizations hold in the field.

The refugee is the participant intellectual who is competent to categorize his situation. Harold Garfinkel used to blame sociologists for considering actors to be cultural idiots following highways of sense. Giving the actor the ability to tell the story of who he or she is, and what he or she stands for, is a fundamental principle. This approach suggests a modest position for the observer. In no way can the researcher be a sort of "director" of the situation. The researcher can never be the leading profile that is going to deliver a semblance of truth to the actor. The academic cannot be, in this concern, the

"*Maestro*" of the situation, conquering the subject of the field. Ironically, the modesty that is required of the researcher was more prevalent at the time of Evans-Pritchard in the 1930s and 1940s than it is nowadays.

The presentation of this theoretical "bricolage" (Lévi-Stauss, 1962) would be incomplete if we did not add the inductive method of the social networks. The errors suggested by these theories were, nonetheless, very useful to re-think our incapacity to find a global theory for forced migration. This weakness has been very much emphasized in different international scientific gatherings here and there. One of the main issues is the impermanence of the object and its inner fluidity, which constitutes a major obstacle for bringing together a theory that could match the object. The theory of social networks proposes an ensemble of methods and techniques, such as graphs and diagrams, in order to calculate the strategies of the actors by estimating their importance through measuring their centrality or autonomy within a structure. The synthetic vision given by the illustration helps to give these measures.

To us, these representations appeared very artificial in the field of forced migration because they gave fixed identities to a moving process. At the moment that the graph grasped a reality, this reality had already changed. In my view, one of the main reasons for the failure of the social networks theory to explain forced migrations is that the refugee is rarely a strategic actor planning flight out of his country. More likely, he or she is in an urgent situation, his or her flight is an escape (*sauve-qui-peut* or runaway flight) rather than an organized voyage. The emergency aspect of the displacement is an important element.

The theory of social networks was, nevertheless, very fruitful for studying other migrations such as pilgrimages or student migrations. In situations where action is planned and organized in advance by the actors, such a theory can be favorable to research and the clarification of intentions, the set of conscious or unconscious goals of the actors. Such a theory helps explain a strategy-like situation where a student, for example, transforms his or her study project into a long-term migration process or an opportunity to discover other worlds.

After presenting all these theoretical "inter-breedings" and all these borrowings of explanations from different disciplines one might realize the polymorphology and the polyvalence of forced migration studies. It might appear as a "Spanish tavern" *("auberge espagnole")* or as a patchwork where one finds whatever one seeks, which very much reflects the reality of an experimental field that has not yet proved to be a sustainable project in the French academic world. The patchwork is also the result of experimental research with no fixed dogmatism.

I would then propose that this new academic field possesses the qualities of its defects. Although innovative, it is at the same time weak from an academic point of view. Re-enforcing the field would be an invitation to investigate the methodologies further and encourage research to go beyond monographs of ethnic communities. Current research is very much limited to scanning ethnic communities in Cairo, and elsewhere, in a very descriptive and empirical approach.

For this reason, I have underlined the importance of a comparative approach in order to escape the imprisonment of the object. Comparative analysis, symbolic interactionism and social network theory inspired this "*bricolage,*" but the list would be incomplete if we did not add all the theoretical approaches of the American anthropologists.

Toward an Anthropology of Suffering

Among the many studies analyzing the consequences of a stressful field on the ethnographer and on the ethnography itself, the collective publication *Fieldwork Under Fire*, edited by Carolyn Nordstrom and Antonius Robben (1984), is of major interest. The study was a pioneering and very stimulating attempt to analyse the multiplicity of implications of a violent field on observers, and the impact of suffering on writing an ethnography. John Davis also gave us a theory of an "anthropology of suffering" by making a distinction between a "balanced" field and a field with abnormal violence (1992). Barbara Harrell-Bond takes an important place among those pioneering researchers by insisting on the specificity of suffering.

Traditionally historians, geographers, and political scientists do not discuss their place in the process of research and are generally advised not to speak about the emotional side of their professional activity. The originality of the above anthropology is that ethical conflicts are now voiced as issues where, most of the time, these dilemmas have remained unspoken in the academic world. Now challenges and dilemmas are all submitted to critical views. For example, the "danger" of having empathy transformed into activism is often discussed in academic debates. Thus, we can also mention intellectual honesty in the ways that inner difficulties are expressed in building these ethnographies.

The "danger" connected with such fields are then experienced by the observers, and often the cruelty of the situation they have to face challenges their vision of life and even their cultural values. Gudrun Kroner underlined this aspect in a CEDEJ workshop in 2001 when comparing Refugee Studies with Palestinian Studies in terms of unbearable violence and profound distress. As a researcher it is difficult to ignore this challenge and not reflect on the specificity of the scientific position in its demand for distance. Profound distress felt by the populations we study has a profound impact on ethnographers.

Another challenge is to admit the relation of the academic object and the position of the researcher. As anthropological literature has always told us, we know that there is never a chance or hazard that a researcher is related to the subject. The existence of a *"mimétisme"* (unconscious imitation) or what can be called a confusion between the academic purpose and the researcher needs to be discussed honestly. There is such suffering in the field of forced migrations that it is impossible for the researcher to remain completely distant and clearly objective.

In Sudan I was very often completely submerged by the suffering of the refugees, and I remember the countless times when my emotions were more powerful than my academic distance. Tears and dry anger were the reactions I had in Sudan many times in the company of informants. One of the most painful memories was when I was accompanying one of my refugee friends who was seeking to be resettled in Australia.

Mulu, an Ethiopian refugee, had heard that the immigration agent from the Australian embassy in Cairo was in Khartoum for few days. Rumors in the refugee community had it that this agent was staying in the most luxurious hotel in Khartoum. Mulu asked me to come with him to the hotel in order to set up a meeting with the agent. We had waited for the bureaucrat for three hours when we heard from the receptionist that he had left the hotel for another one. I wrote a letter to the agent asking for an appointment, explaining Mulu's case. That letter never received an answer, and I remember with acute pain the feeling of being of no account: something not worth being heard. For the first time I understood emotionally what it was to be a refugee, how it was to be voiceless, how it was not to be a somebody, to be a non-being, something to be denied. I remember Mulu's eyes full of tears and I was fighting not to show my own tears.

I remember the feeling of injustice, the feeling of being betrayed by cold bureaucrats despising the basic ethics of life. The power of the institution was proclaiming the insignificance of being a human soul. This experience was a turning point in my research. From that time some kind of emotional flux made me feel "a refugee" myself. Dealing with displaced populations I was becoming *one of them*. One consequence of this state was the kind of reaction my colleagues had to me during that field research. They felt embarrassed by an over-reacting research program, and my moral commitment was a source of misunderstanding. I realized that I was seeing them as "lazy researchers having a vacation in Egypt," attributing to them a bad image of opportunism. During that field research I had but one ear, one voice, and one intelligence who understood what I felt. Barbara Harrell-Bond was a major support and inspiring academic. The rest of the French scientific community in Cairo could not understand the feeling of exclusion I had. I was always accompanied by refugees, I was walking in the streets with black refugees, and I have experienced in my "soul" the racism that the refugees felt, the ordinary stigmatization and scorn. Their suffering became by effect of consequence my suffering. Academics identify this process as "empathy."

The second dramatic experience was in Eritrea in May 2003. I had come to Asmara to seek more information about the Eritrean Beni Amer in the North East of Sudan,[5] where I was taken to the desert to see an abandoned refugee camp (see Chapter Five) in which hundred of refugees were starving. The UNHCR had cut the water pump and the food ration to push them out of Sudan. I filmed the refugees and took pictures while interviewing them about their refusal to go back to Eritrea.

I met the spokesman of the Eritrean president, who rejected the pictures I had taken, claiming it was a lie and that the images had been faked through tendentious editing. I remained speechless and started to cry. I could not stop. The politician was so embarrassed that he did not know what to do. He never expected that emotional reaction. He then withdrew from the first position, telling me that I could not possibly lie, and using his telephone called two or three ministers. A car took me directly to the Ministry of Relief where I met with other politicians who accepted my testimony but remained totally mute about the causes of the refusal of these groups to come back home.

I remember how disappointed and how powerless I felt.

The number of these experiences could be endless and I could write a whole book about the heartrending experience of confronting the cynical attitudes of institutions and politicians. My reaction to cynicism was overacting, over-valuing, over-doing, overestimating, and expressing a very acute sense of guilt, especially in Sudan where materially the refugees were living in extremely difficult economic conditions. I was tempted to become like Mother Teresa; knowing perfectly well that it was a mistake to undertake that particular profile. I could not restrain myself from helping the refugees. I was in Sudan with my private funds. I started to install floors in the huts. I went with my

---

5 On the Beni Amer tribe, see Alberto Pollera, Le popolazioni indigine dell'Eritrea (Bologna: Licino Cappelli, 1935) p. 337. About Eritrean revolution, see John Markakis, National and Class Conflict in the Horn of Africa (Cambridge: Cambridge University Press, 1987) p.

driver to a very large market and brought hundred meters of plastic flooring material for the houses of the refugees. At a certain point I felt exhausted and had to admit that I would not (my little self) change anything. It was like a Herculean duty that I could not humanly achieve. I was not paid for that by my institution, I was not sent to Sudan by an NGO or a church. I was following a research program. This contradiction was a source of suffering for me.

Continuing on the problematic of pain we will first in the next chapter evoke the profound distress of the Ethiopian Diaspora in Cairo. We will see the essence and the fears of a community always on the move, always in a culture of impermanence and transit. We will study spatial instability and forced nomadism in the Egyptian capital.

Chapter 3
Cultural Aspects of the Transient Ethiopian Diaspora in Cairo
Stress, Spatial Instability and Disorders

DERECK COOPER IN 1992 was pioneering in his fieldwork on the "transient essence" of the Ethiopian and Eritrean Diaspora in Cairo (Cooper 1992). Thirteen years after his research, my own conclusions tend to confirm that the Ethiopian and Eritrean presence in Cairo is mainly transient. The reason behind this central statement is rooted in the causes for Abyssinian migrations outside their countries. Forced migrants follow a "circulation territory" from the Sudanese frontier in Kassala to Khartoum, the capital, then to Upper Egypt and finally Cairo. The itinerary is more or less a step-wise migration, reflecting a geographical dynamic that is linked with the valley of the Nile. The Blue Nile has its source in Ethiopia; it runs from there to Sudan and thence to the Mediterranean. From ancient times, the great Nile valley gained its coherence by forming a circulation corridor that is now followed by the forced migrants from Ethiopia in noticeable numbers.

The main reason for the Abyssinian influx in Sudan in their first step of migration is directly related to two centuries of political and climatic instability. Since 1961, Ethiopia and Eritrea have been nearly continually at war. Seven years after Eritrean independence from Ethiopia in 1991, brothers and enemies rose against one another in another conflict over their common frontier (Le Houérou, 2000). Chronic instability in these two very poor countries has unceasingly produced refugees. Escaping this instability is very logical behavior. In Sudan, all the Ethiopians and Eritreans we interviewed were willing to be resettled abroad and had come to Khartoum for this specific reason. In Cairo, most refugees describe similar motivations. To reach Western countries and to be resettled in America, Australia, or Canada is a commonly-shared dream in the African Diasporas in Cairo.

Much evidence shows that only a few migrants fulfill that dream (Kuhlman, 1990, 1994). Field research in Khartoum proved very clear on this point. Resettlement programs will never match the expectations of refugees. Thousands of files are pending, waiting to be studied by immigration officers in the main embassies. Officers of certain countries only come to Khartoum from time to time, so the waiting list for the resettlement program in the Sudanese capital is interminable. More than 50,000 urban refugees are bogged down in static situations, dreaming of further migrations. Yet, despite having lived in the country for lengthy periods, they remain hopeful that one day they will be resettled, thus maintaining the permanent myth of their transit passage through Sudan. The paradox in Sudan is their long exile in the country and the existence of a durable transient mentality. Waiting for the verdict of the immigration administration can be agonizing, as I was continually reminded during my fieldwork in Sudan.

Figure 1: **Resettlement (Khartoum)**

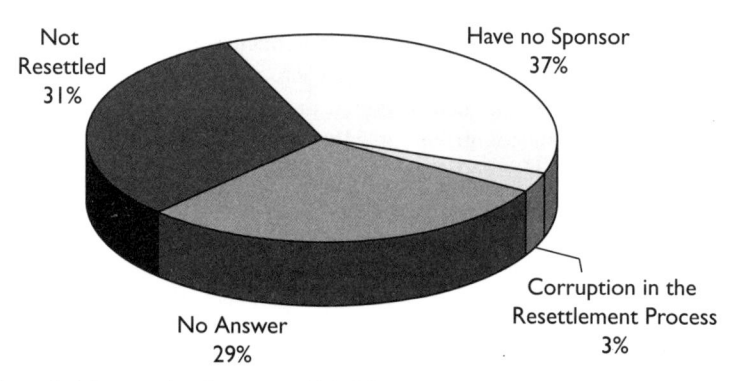

- Not Resettled 31%
- Have no Sponsor 37%
- Corruption in the Resettlement Process 3%
- No Answer 29%

All the graphs below are taken from an unpublished document presented by the author in a seminar at the CEDEJ, Cairo, March 2003

The same paradox is to be observed in Cairo. In the Egyptian capital, most informants arrived in Egypt through Sudan and considered the stop in Cairo as a short interlude before further migrations. In fact, based on my interviews, 99 percent of them wanted to leave Egypt. The furtive essence of this passage has many consequences in terms of social organization. We explored the effects and impacts of this transit aspect in the Diaspora in

Cairo: the way people live and are rooted in the urban space; and the ways identities are reshaped in the process of building their territory in a megalopolis like Cairo.

The majority of informants for this research were young male deserters from the Ethiopian and Eritrean armies and a group of young females employed as domestic workers in Cairo. Most of them live illegally in the urban setting. This absence of juridical status has a direct and very clear consequence on refugees' attitudes. Absence of rights induces absence of stability. After interviewing hundreds of refugees in Cairo, Barbara Harrell-Bond concluded that no improvement in the refugees' situation could ever happen without legal recognition. In response to the need, she established a legal aid program in Cairo. Her conclusion was confirmed in a report drawn up by Forced Migration and Refugee Studies (FMRS) students under her direction (Brown et al, 2003). Research conducted in this field has indicated a correlation between the permanence of movement and a life lived in a state of continuous fear. After analyzing this fear and the multiplicity of consequences of "being scared" and "being terrorized," this chapter presents an anthropological interpretation of fear. It enumerates the main consequences of that emotional state on the social organization of the group in Cairo in order to appreciate the powerful influence of an emotional state on the social life of that particular group.

Figure 2: **Ethiopian/Eritrean Refugees in Cairo: Gender Identification**

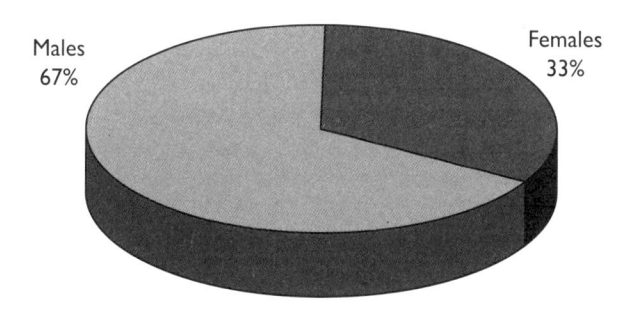

Movement under the Shadow of Fear

Numerous sources justify this interpretation of fear (Cooper, 1992; Harrell-Bond, 2002; Le Houérou, 2004). The legal aid program launched by Harrell-Bond in Cairo in 2000 confirms that, in all aspects, refugee asylum seekers and refugees have fears concerning their presence in the Egyptian capital.

Beyond the question of aid, recognition of rights remains the priority for people on the move. The absence of any legal status puts an individual in a very fragile position and engenders a strong feeling of insecurity. This anxiety has multiple consequences on the life of the refugee. It is not a local feeling without social and historical implications.

Living in fear provokes a harmful social isolation. The fear of being arrested shapes the way bodies move in the city, thus highlighting the problem of place for the refugee. In this concern, they build their territories as isolated "islands," thus escaping from common interaction. Fear provokes social and psychological damage as well. It can overwhelm a person. Fear has psychological effects on people's interaction with the world, as everyday life and contact with others comes to be seen as a risk.

For the purposes of this account we shall first give a global estimate of the Ethiopian and Eritrean populations in Cairo. As mentioned above, Dereck Cooper conducted his research in 1992. At that time he estimated the size of the community as from 700 to more than 1,000 souls. Today, we estimate that Abyssinians are between 5,000 and 10,000 people. During a personal survey well-informed, confidential sources estimated the size of the Ethiopian and Eritrean Diaspora in Cairo as comparable to that of the Somalis, and a young Somali researcher once gave a rough estimate of about 6,000 Somali refugees in Cairo (al-Sharmani, 2003). The Somali communities are relatively small in comparison with the Sudanese. Providing an accurate measure of the Sudanese presence in Cairo is almost impossible. Most extravagant numbers are touted in the media, but, as far as refugees are concerned, the real number of Southerners in Cairo probably does not exceed 60,000. A common rumor alludes to 100,000 asylum seekers. This, of course, does not take into account the numbers of Northern immigrants from Sudan.

Interviews with Ethiopian migrants were conducted in various Cairo neighborhoods: New Maadi, Mohandessin, Dokki, Heliopolis, and Shubra. For this purpose we travelled to the five locales. The main group of informants were of Amhara and Tigrinya (Eritrea) origin and had escaped national service. More than any other group amongst this Diaspora, deserters and draft evaders struggled with stress and personal disorders. In Eritrea there is also an obligatory 18-month military service for women. Informant testimonies are unanimous about the harshness of this, not only in a physical sense but also mentally. Not only were girls forced to participate in very heavy public utility works, but they were also submitted to harsh rules in terms of discipline in order to "break the character" of any critical mind. Physical harassment, punishment, and humiliation were the main examples informants described.

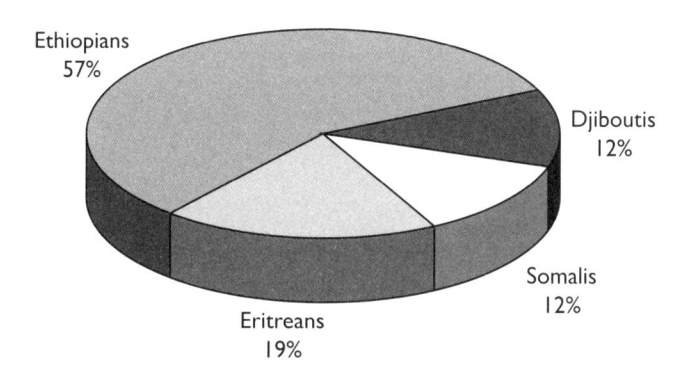

Figure 3: Number of refugees by nationalities (Cairo)

- Ethiopians 57%
- Eritreans 19%
- Somalis 12%
- Djiboutis 12%

The subject of national service provoked horror among those Eritreans interviewed in Cairo. Among this group, a remarkable percentage of young men were university students who had deferred their military service. In discussing their motivation to escape, they very often mentioned the fear of having to fight against Ethiopia once again. We must recall that Ethiopia and Eritrea have been at war for almost half a century; first, in a civil war between 1961 and 1991; then, after Eritrea gained its independence in 1991, the new state again fought Ethiopia in 1998, a bloody two-year border war that ended in a peace deal signed in Algiers in December 2000 (Le Houérou, 2000). According to the press, the war cost nearly 100,000 lives. After the peace agreement, the two countries progressed toward a very fragile peace, but Ethiopia is contesting the demarcation of the 1,000-kilometer border in Badme and over parts of the Irob area. The zone remains vulnerable and many observers consider that the peace process is continuously challenged. Fears have grown that in the absence of a breakthrough, tensions between Eritrea and Ethiopia could once again flare up in a resumption of hostilities. Peace is thus at risk.

The fear of having to run from another war also motivates the evaders. This unpopular war inspires horror on both sides. Ethiopian and Eritrean informants emphasize their cultural similarities. In an exiled territory in Sudan or in Cairo, many refugees would identify the two groups as being very much alike if compared with other African nationalities: alike in the ways of speaking, eating, and behaving.

The risk of a new war is one of the causes of inner panic expressed by this particular group. Ironically, this group is rejected on a major scale by the United Nations High Commissioner for Refugees (UNHCR), the institution that is in charge of status determination. Only two informants were recognized as refugees by UNHCR. I have observed that most of these young deserters were so stressed that they were unable to defend themselves, even if their motives were informed by issues of conscience, as they were conscientious objectors. In a state of shock, these young men were hardly able to convince the UNHCR Protection Officers of the causes of their evasion. In this context, we again emphasize the effectiveness and importance of the legal aid program, which was the right tool to challenge UN "narrowness" on this particular point. One task of the legal aid program is to help the asylum seeker make a formal effort to present his demand for status determination at the UNHCR office. Most evaders feared to declare themselves as deserters. In simplistic terms, the UNHCR often responded to a person's agitated state by considering him a liar, and thus rejected his claim, instead of recognizing the state of panic. The legal aid program has been a useful medium to advise asylum seekers to tell the truth during the process of status determination. It advises the seeker to sincerely express his motives for refusing to participate in a war.

These young men arrive in Cairo already traumatized by their past experience in the army. In the Egyptian capital, they lock themselves in apartments that are rented collectively. In the first months after arrival they try to avoid any kind of interaction with Egyptian society because they fear deportation to the Sudanese desert, a tragic end that would mean imprisonment (in the best case) or other punishment, including capital punishment as stressed by some informants. For them, deportation is a matter of life and death. The immense risk of arrest is thus one of the reasons to avoid outside life.

The city appears as a place full of danger. This anxiety was observed in the group as a common bond between the young men. Acute fear leads to a social paralytic state that can be a serious handicap for the person. Fear is a negative emotional bond and a common experience that links the men together. Most of them declare themselves to be depressed. Much has been reported about post-traumatic stress disorders (PTSD) related to refugees. In our current field research, two manifestations of this PTSD were sleeping all day or watching television day and night. The impact of terrifying visions takes a long time to disappear, as expressed by Abraham: "I keep in my body the stigma of fear." The young man is constantly looking over his shoulder and scanning the city streets, espying the urban environment to seek security in his daily goings-on. The urban environment is therefore a place to be feared. In urban studies, the place of the refugees within the urban setting is rarely a subject of study. Any description of the movement of these wanderers would emphasize the extraordinary anxiety accompanying any singular and casual movement. Circulation in the city for members of that group, and other refugees, is thus a terrifying enterprise. Deserters are perhaps the most vulnerable, but they are not the only group paralyzed with fear when forced to move.

To be Scared in the City, to be Scared of the City

It is difficult for a free person to imagine the effort that an "illegal" person has to make to accomplish the simplest movement in an urban space. Ordinary movement provokes belly-aches or sweat. Only direct observation of the group can really measure the devastating impact of fright. Below is one woman's account of how even shopping was becoming a source of drama for her:

> *I'm scared everywhere: even when I do some shopping. I never come back home after 6 pm. I never feel at ease. Never. I had a lot of chance because I will be resettled in Australia. Before the resettlement I lived under oppressive fear for five years. This fear does not disappear in one day! It takes ages to disappear. Every time I travel, the fear comes back. The fear is in my blood. Sometimes I have the feeling that this fear is rooted in my cells.*

Figure 4: **Depression among Refugees in Cairo**

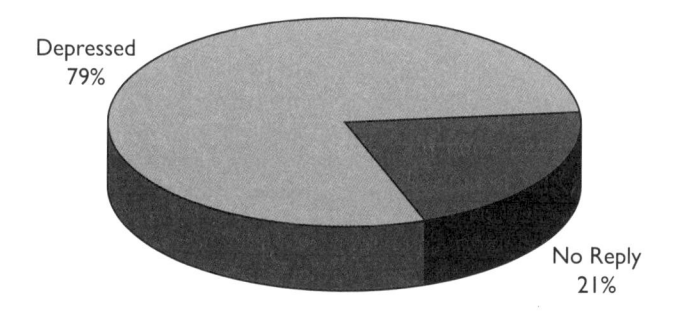

Depressed 79%
No Reply 21%

This very stirring confession shows the devastating power of fright. "Almaz" confessed that she only realized the sharpness of this inner panic when she was resettled. It was only when she was reassured about her future life that she could analyze all the changes in her personality that had been provoked by extreme fright. One consequence of her fright was an avoidance response to any deep commitment. She was suspicious of the whole city and she refused to commit herself to any affectionate relationship. She declared that she would agree to marry only when resettled in Australia. She also confessed that she did not want to have any children unless she was sure she would have "a second chance in Australia." Many refugee women said they practiced birth control. Among 150 interviewees, we recorded only ten children. One of the most tragic consequences of this fear is the limitation it imposes on the individual's insertion into his or her own community and the resulting refusal to create any meaningful link.

An absence of links puts people into a limbo-type situation. Ironically, perhaps, it is only when they have finished the process of resettlement that they feel free to talk about it. In other words, refugees started to talk about their fears only when those fears started to fade.

One side effect of the fear of living in the city is continuously to move house. Even for fully legalized refugees, the city is always seen as a threat. Hussein, interviewed in the 2003 documentary "*Nomads and Pharaohs,*"[1] said he had changed his house 10 times in three years. On average, informants changed their residence three times a year. Residential instability is a side effect of that profound fear of being arrested. There is a chronic instability inherent in city life. Thus refugees should be seen as urban nomads always seeking a sense of security. Their movements have to be understood in terms of searching for a refuge, a hiding place to be hidden from the eyes of others, a search for invisibility.

As far as the Abyssinian highlanders are concerned, this nomadic habit is imposed by the situation. Amhara and Tigrinya are peasants who are very much rooted to their land. For them, residential instability is not part of their culture as it might be for other ethnic groups. Moving from one apartment to another is not the result of choice or style; rather, it is made necessary by a life lived under the weight of fear. The global change, in this context imposed by forced exile, is extremely violent. The paradox is that the young men are locked in their places without moving, but at the same time are always on the move in search of "another place."

This unbalanced relation concerning movement is specific to army evaders and deserters and can be considered as a structural characteristic of their group. The constant moving can be part of an anthropology of movement under the emotional state of fear; a situation related to the absence of any

---

1 "Nomads and Pharaohs" is a documentary film (46 minutes) directed by Fabienne Le Houérou in 2003 for TV5, CNRS. The film explores the relations between refugees and their hosts through a set of interactions. It illustrates the theoretical value of the concept of the gift as studied by Mauss.

rights. This movement is stigmatizing. No other group of refugees in the city shows such a pathological relation to the space. Nor is this group's residential instability comparable to other poor in the capital. Poor Egyptians can at least be protected by the national authority and can move freely.

Casual common sense would suggest that the absence of freedom of movement is one of the most terrible things a human being can experience, being comparable to a prison-like situation. In many cases, informants described their situation as a "jail situation" in which the young men were their own jailers, imposing on themselves a jail-like discipline. One interpretation I am tempted to give is that of ex-soldiers from a totalitarian institution (Goffman, 1968); these young men were still under the shock of their previous experience in the army so that they over-emphasized the danger in a city like Cairo.

Figure 5: Job Opportunities in Cairo

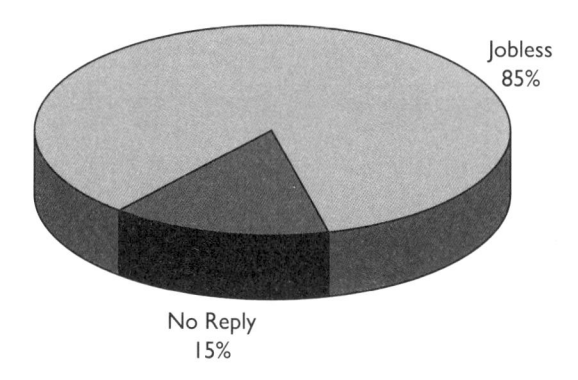

Jobless 85%

No Reply 15%

Comparison is, thus, heuristic with other African communities. It seems that, despite living with the same absence of rights, Sudanese refugees in the Arba'a wa-Nus neighborhood of Cairo do not voice their fears of being arrested with comparable strength. Even if the risk of arrest is rational, the evaluation of that risk is very much over-emphasized. Army punishments also seemed to inspire major panic. As far as I am aware, Eritrean and Ethiopian jails are not shining examples of human rights institutions. On the contrary, deserters taken back to Eritrea fear they may face torture in prison. It remains very difficult to measure the degree of violence of the military system in that country. What we know comes from Amnesty International, which has reported on the miserable conditions of detainees. Cases of torture have been reported in Ethiopia, and Ethiopian asylum seekers in Cairo corroborate this information (Brown et al, 2003). In Eritrea, the punishment for desertion is extremely severe, as stated by interviewees. The harshness of the treatment in the army is confirmed again by the FMRS report concerning Ethiopian and Eritrean insecurity in Cairo (Brown et al, 2003:12). Cases of torture are too frequently reported for us not to take them into account. Repeated beating on the feet is quite a common punishment, even for women. One informant in Cairo was raped during conscription. In Cairo, she was renting a flat with a fellow who also escaped the army. It was many months before she could speak again. She related that she remained almost mute for many months and was so scared to go out in the street that she did not want to go to the UNHCR office. She appealed to the UN office only after two years in Cairo.

Figure 6: **Activities of the Refugees in Cairo**

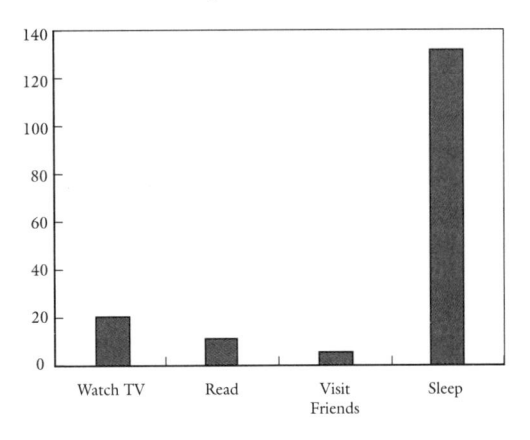

The group analyzed here exhibits all the evidence of suffering beyond the normal or common. Undertaking fieldwork with such a population is comparable to constructing an ethnography of suffering (Davis, 1992). Members of the group live under emotional stress and suffer PTSD. Their symptoms are similar to those expressed by American soldiers who fought in the Vietnam war. The US National Center for Post Traumatic Disorder demonstrated that PTSD can provoke brain damage and other physical changes. Scientists have stressed that victims of devastating trauma may never be the same biologically, as shown by Dennis Charney, a Yale psychologist who researched the biological impact of uncontrollable stress (Charney et al, 1999; Duman and Charney, 1999), and research centers have analyzed these disorders in laboratory rats. Researchers focused mainly on the feeling of helplessness, that the feeling that "there is nothing you can do" constitutes an overwhelming emotional response to any given event. The conscripted girl who was raped had very painful headaches; she complained of "losing her mind" and "forgetting everything." Her statements aptly illustrate the impact of horror on memory.

I will study the "loss of history" and memory among refugees in Sudan and in Cairo in Chapter Six. The aim of the next chapter is to recall the studies of French philosopher Henri Bergson and his conclusions about the "pathology of memory" (Bergson, 1939). He analyzed the process of the loss of memory in relation to drama. He concluded that a traumatic shock could provoke memory failure. In terms of an individual's memory, his theory suggested the existence of a pure memory. In terms of a collective group, one could ask: What are the consequences of such loss of memory? When thousands of people present the same symptoms vis-à-vis memory loss, it is quite important that academic research understands more about this process. One concrete consequence of memory loss among the refugees studied, and related to their survival mechanisms, was the loss of self-defense strategies. The Beni Amer Eritreans in Kassala region constitute a paradigm of this (Le Houérou, 2003). Horrors harmed their memory and elicited a "freeze" response in future confrontations. Refugees refused to repatriate to their country because of this altered memory (Le Houérou, 2004).

Figure 7: **Relation of the Refugees with their Landlords in Cairo**

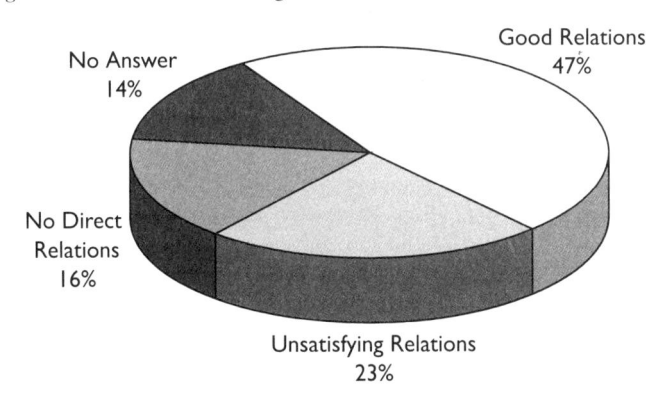

- Good Relations 47%
- Unsatisfying Relations 23%
- No Direct Relations 16%
- No Answer 14%

As mentioned above, military deserters from a military state like Eritrea are not the only "movers" in Cairo to express chronic residential instability. One of my key informants returned to his country of origin as soon as the political situation was suitable.

> *Here [in Cairo] I will always live like a starving rat, going out at night to get the garbage of a society that only tolerates me if I am discrete and nice. People bear with us only as disabled humans.*

He was expressing a wish to be someone, to have a "normal place" with a "normal life" and a "respectable position." He confessed that he always felt out of place even if he was working and had a relatively comfortable financial situation. Even as a recognized refugee—not having to fear deportation—this lack of place was the main complaint he made about his life in Cairo. Perhaps this explains why some refugees sometimes pretend to be diplomats. They believe that African diplomats are the only black people who are really comfortable in Cairo. The position of a diplomat is socially recognized. The refugees' Egyptian hosts see the forced migrants more as ambassadors of poverty.

Figure 8: **UNHCR Status**

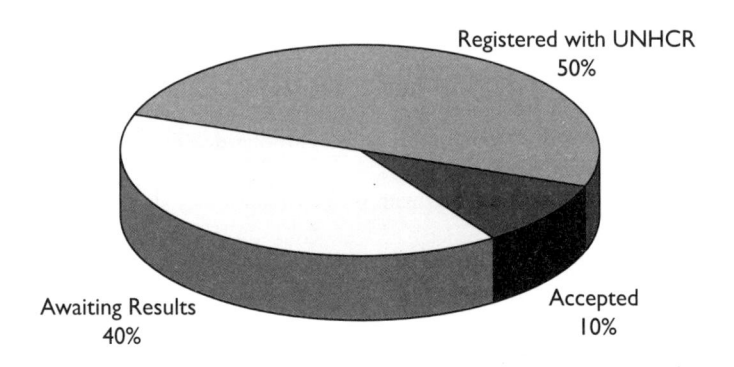

Registered with UNHCR 50%
Awaiting Results 40%
Accepted 10%

We have an interaction of fear, between army evaders who fear arrest, and Egyptian society that fears waves of poor people "bringing problems and diseases." This type of interaction resembles what is observed in Western countries. The combination of these fears leads—sometimes—to terrible misunderstandings that only hinder the integration process. Female refugees express a fear of being operated on in an Egyptian hospital because of their belief in the existence of a market for stolen organs. This urban myth has been exaggerated, but fears can be transformed into social facts—even if based only on a myth. Fears are also the product of concrete realities, and even if the danger is over-stated it should be taken seriously. Sometimes myths have proved more powerful than memories. Myths are not as fragile as historical representations and are very difficult to refute.

To conclude, the legal aid program in Cairo[2] has been a good response to the condition of "helplessness" of this particular group. Giving refugees legal tools to defend themselves also gives them a place where they can they can re-conquer their dignity so as to find a place in the host society. Legal aspects can not be separated from the anthropological analysis of their fears in the context of war in Ethiopia/Eritrea. This vulnerability also challenges our ways at looking at gender differences in exile. As army evaders, young Ethiopian and Eritrean men were much more stressed than women. Here again, ethnic solidarity proved to result from a gender revolution. Women in Cairo were actually protecting the men. As we attempted to demonstrate, army deserters form what can be considered a "vulnerable group." This vulnerability should never be studied beyond its context. The conditions of flight are the root causes of this vulnerability and we will insist that measuring such a notion is not possible. This is also a reason why academics are useful when challenging the jargon of the humanitarian actors. By labelling groups, they give them a definitive identity as "irregular movers" or "vulnerable groups." Why should women and children be the only vulnerable categories? No definitive statement can be cast in this concern. Men, under certain conditions, can prove to be as helpless as children. Juridical categories always fail because they tend to give a-historical definitions and, in the context of migrations and forced migrations, fixed identities lead to a theoretical dead-end. Identities of people should be interpreted as moving processes. Ironically, aid agencies are imposing juridical concepts and approaches, thus reducing movement within a limited legal structure.

Fearing the outside world, voluntary self-imprisonment, is the main consequence of the illegal status for these populations on the move in the Egyptian capital. The suffering of these urban nomads is very different from the painful experience of refugees outside the urban settings. We will see in the next pages how specific interactions between aid workers and refugees in Sudanese refugee camps can add dramatically to the risk for the refugee population. In these camps the Ethiopian and Eritrean refugees are living under norms created and imposed by the UN agencies.

---

2 A legal laid program was created by Barbara Harrell-Bond in Cairo. From 2000 to 2005 hundreds of asylum seekers were heard by volunteers and lawyers in order to prepare and defend their cases in a juridical way in front of the UNHCR officers. I had the privilege to participate to this very useful program for eight months.

Chapter 4
Painful Interactions between Humanitarian Actors and Their Clients
Blond Angels and the Refugees in the Sudanese Desert

REFUGEES AND FORCED MIGRANTS exist in an unbalanced relationship with humanitarian organizations and academics. This relationship has already been the topic of academic research. Mark Walkup in the *Journal of Refugee Studies* in 1997 describes the dysfunctions in humanitarian organizations and "the role of coping strategies among humanitarian actors." A number of the dysfunctions that Walkup identified are based on insolvable ethical issues that humanitarian actors are forced to face. The personnel of humanitarian organizations (HO) cope with a number of internal conflicts that arise due to the dichotomy between the declared principles of their institutions and the everyday reality in the field. In another article published in the *Human Rights Quarterly* in 2002, Barbara Harrell-Bond asks the question, "Can humanitarian work with refugees be humane?" She analyzes the asymmetrical relationship between helpers and receivers. She argues that the social context for giving assistance puts refugees in an inferior position.

This empirical evidence can be verified in any kind of humanitarian-type relationship. Givers are omnipotent, while receivers are in a supplicant position. A documentary film shot in Cairo, Khartoum and Kassala explores these types of unbalanced relationships according to the universal Maussian pattern of "giving, receiving, and reciprocating" ("Nomads and Pharoahs"). But how can we expect a refugee moving through a foreign urban environment to give anything back?

In my own field research, like many other scholars, I continuously faced this violent contrast of superordinate and subordinate positions. Charity can be violent and insulting in terms of human dignity. Authority and charity are very tightly linked: one hand dictates while the other hand gives. In fact, they have been coupled at least since the European Middle Ages. The Church symbolized charity, while the State embodied political authority. The Church-State coupling worked to help each other. Nowadays, charity activity is mainly the heir of the Church's sacred task to care for the poor. The succession is historically marked in France. Before the French Revolution, churches carried the social burden. Caring for the sick, orphans and disabled was traditionally the task of the Church, but the Revolution completely secularized charity. Consciously or unconsciously humanitarian organizations are the heirs of such charitable traditions. This sacred heritage was crystallized in a particular moment during my field research in Sudan.

Heroes and Refugees

When I was in the Sita wa-'Ishrin camp in Gédaref state (Eastern Sudan), a Beni Amer lady originally from Eritrea rushed to me, kissing my hands and calling me a "*blond angel.*" I remember how I categorically rejected being identified in that way. Later, with critical distance, I realised that this lady had assumed that I belonged to a World Food Program project working in Shagarab. The term "blond angel" was used to denote all the staff from Western countries. The refugees viewed staff as heroes or divine messengers, powerful and able to provide protection just like the heroes in ancient Greek myths. Thus, the relationship between the refugees and humanitarian actors was much more than asymmetrical; it was a relationship based on almost "sacred" assumptions. Humanitarian actors were more than human, they were super-human; "*heroized*" in the classical sense of the term. They were not gods; but, nonetheless, they were superior to regular human beings. They stood a little above humanity.

I inquired further about how refugees perceived the aid staff. The message was clear: they were sent by God to the camp in order to help, to protect, and to distribute the food rations, thereby deciding who ate, when they ate, and how much they ate. The priority of food meant that the status of food distributors became similar to that of doctors: they are both unconditional saviours.

I remember how uncomfortable I felt cast in this mythical and false image. It created such an inner sense of rebellion in me that I was surprised to see how delighted the HO agent was to know that refugees called her a "*blond angel.*" For her, the image confirmed her positive role. Undoubtedly, she was a very professional and committed member of the staff. She was, however, viewed critically by her colleagues because she wore elegant suits even when monitoring in the desert of Sita wa-'Ishrin: in the dust and "*khamsin*" wind she never changed her very chic style. She did not wear the traditional basketball shoes or blue jeans like her colleagues, and did not fit in with the style of the main group. It was not what was expected in a camp in the desert. Beliefs concerning what is suitable or not, correct or not, create common values and culture. These are the conscious or unconscious links that bond the HO community together. There exist common values and common ways of seeing the world and even common ways to dress and common ways of evaluating image. Reaction to the blond angel exemplifies perfectly the culture and attitudes that are taken for granted in such a field.

On the refugee side, I happen to know that in another camp, one that was better organised and where a number of NGO's were operating, this same HO agent had a nickname: she was called "Barbie"[1] by the refugees. Nevertheless, the refugees respected her and were using a much nicer way to make fun of her than were her colleagues. You might wonder why I pause to consider the different labels that refugees give to an HO staff member. Is it not a detail of little or no importance? Why describe such interaction between the "blond angel" and the refugees? How is this of interest to an academic? Is "*ethnographing*"[2] an agent from an HO a legitimate pursuit? This question could raise ethical issues.

In my opinion, including a humanitarian worker in an ethnography requires a common cosmogony and shared symbols. Furthermore, such an ethnography casts light on the sacred relationship between the refugees and the "blond angel" and the myth of efficiency and vital importance of the job. To be put on such a "pedestal" suggests that the individual stands above question. This elevated position does not allow for critique. Referring back to the absolute savior motif, biblical stories and Greeks myths alike stress that mortals cannot critically assess the divine. This pedestal, therefore, does not

---

1 There are copies of Barbie dolls in Sudanese markets of towns such as Gadaref and Kassala. The imitation of the American toy is made out a very cheap plastic, has blond hair and blue eyes.

2 The Barbie doll can also be seen as a cultural symbol in the North American perspective.

allow for any kind of ethnographic approach and would probably make such a study appear as a transgression, or even sin.

The studies of Harrell-Bond gave a formidable push for the need to have a wider research approach than the classical vertical analysis of humanitarian organisations. Reading *Imposing Aid* (1986) was intellectually refreshing and represented an academic liberation from stereotyped assumptions. It was an innovative move in classical research methodology to study migrations while underlining some fundamentally fuzzy aspects of the forced migrations.

I observed in Sudan that HO staff generally agree to be "heroized" and accept the profile of savior. They are ready to assume a parental type of authority. HO agents (but it is also true for other workers in HO) are seen as one family. "Father" and "mother" are words refugees often use to identify the institutions dealing with them. Sometimes they even sing it when an important member of the institution from Geneva comes for a visit. By accepting this role, the HO puts the refugee in an infantile position. Refugees, in turn, become the "babies" of the agencies. Refugees place total trust in the institution. They assume that the HO staff will choose what is best for them, just as children trust their parents. As institutions remain, after all, institutions and therefore theoretical bodies and power organisations, these roles inevitably lead to abuse.

Total Trust Leads to Total Disaster

Refugees I met in Kassala Province, particularly members of the Eritrean Beni Amer, never doubted that the HO would always provide the necessary food and water supplies for them. Old refugees, in Sudan since the 1960s, never thought they would one day be forced to repatriate. On December 31, 2002, the UNHCR ended refugee status for Eritreans who had fled their country because of the war of independence in Eritrea or because of the latest conflict between Ethiopia and Eritrea. Once applied, the concrete consequences were the closure of many refugee camps.

There are 223,000 Eritreans remaining in Sudan. Of these, 92,000 live in refugee camps while the rest are assumed to reside in urban areas. Some 100,000 have already returned home; 50,000 of them with UNHCR assistance. Another 32,000 have registered to go home, but their return was prevented owing to political tensions between Sudan and Eritrea.

A large group, however, refuses to repatriate. According to the UNHCR office in Asmara, which wrote to me in April 2003 in response to an article that I had written for *Le Monde Diplomatique*, 150,000 refugees had applied for Refugee Status determination (RSD) and 30 percent would be accepted. I was told that 12 teams of 60 Protection Officers (mainly Egyptians) were interviewing the refugees and that this enormous exercise would continue until June 2003. I was assured there would be "no forced repatriation."

In three camps in Kassala Province (Um Gulsa, New Shegarab and Laffa), Eritrean refugees refused to go home. They number more than 8,000, according to NGO and Sudanese authorities (COR). The majority are Beni Amer. I visited the camps in March 2002 during my field research and filmed the refugees as part of the documentary process. Although the images were shot with a very small digital camera and cannot, therefore, be considered a film, the images remain a direct, non-constructed document dealing, in a very rudimentary way, with unbearable human suffering.

In order to move the Eritreans out of the camp, the water pump was removed. The action did not constitute a clear expulsion of the people. There was no army and no tanks. But it did constitute an indirect invitation to people to leave the camp if they wished to drink potable water. Schools and hospitals were closed and an international organisation asked an NGO in Khartoum to "clear out the camp," according to one informant (Le Houérou, 2003).

These actions can be construed as blackmail: a bargain for food ration and water supply. When the "blond angel" starts blackmailing, a nightmare ensues. When the camp was closed, the children ran to the Gash River to dig the mud for water. I saw an old man near death and witnessed many illnesses. The consequences of cutting the water supply were terrible. When I asked the workers responsible in Kassala why these people were left without any support, the response I repeatedly heard was: "They are no longer refugees; they have to go!"

Article 34 of the Geneva Convention says that the "contracting states shall, as far as possible, facilitate the assimilation and naturalisation of refugees. They shall in particular make every effort to expedite naturalisation proceedings and to reduce as far as possible the charges or costs of such proceedings." I have not heard of such efforts being undertaken in Kassala, particularly not for the Beni Amer, a nomadic tribe who, for centuries, used to cross the border freely. Members of this tribe should obtain Sudanese nationality quite easily because of the historical and kinship links they share with the Sudanese Beni Amer.

When I went to Eritrea to conduct further investigations in May 2002, the same position was reiterated: "They are not refugees anymore!" The UNHCR office considered the political situation between Eritrea and Ethiopia stable; yet IRIN, a UN News agency, warned regularly about the fragility of the peace process since the Algiers Agreement in 2000, and IRIN reported that the borders were insecure. I asked a member of the Eritrean government about the situation of these people. I was told, "It is not true! There are no Eritreans living in such conditions." At the Eritrean relief agency (ERREC), employees did not help much: they advised me that, if I was a researcher, I should do more research! Then they suggested that these people could be Islamists or fundamentalists belonging to the Eritrean Jihad. So, their first response was to accuse me of lying, and their second response was to accuse the refugees of being dangerous.

I was then subjected to symbolic violence due to the images I had taken. My treatment absolutely violated all ethical principles about protection. The images wounded the government's national pride. Because it was deemed not possibly true that a "blond angel" could blackmail a vulnerable ex-refugee group and that the Eritrean government remained mute, it was easier to blame the academic.

An international organization responded rigidly, and with much jargon, to my observations about a human disaster. According to the organization, cutting rations to encourage people to evacuate a region was "voluntary repatriation." In their coping strategies, HO personnel adopted what Walkup identifies as the third stage strategy in which the staff blame others: politics, donors, refugees or, in my circumstance, an academic. They censure the victims as the "villains," as Barbara Harrell-Bond commented in *Imposing Aid* (Harrell-Bond, 1986:436). In this case, the HO and the state placed the blame on the researcher in order to protect the cultural myths of the organization and the national pride of the state.

Myths are created to justify action. My images of the plight of the refugees challenged two myths: the HO myths of efficiency and of being saviors on a sacred mission, and the national myth of the Eritrean State and its relation with the Diaspora and the sacred right to return. The latter strikes at the heart of the problem, that of the "hierarchy of return," to use a term Rina Isotolo[3] (2001) uses for Palestinian refugees. Are all Eritreans on an equal footing when they return home? Is there any ethnic issue with a tribe that is mainly to be found in the refugee camps of Sudan? Why do 65 percent of the people in those camps belong to the same tribe? Is it, by chance, that this tribe was the main support of the Eritrean Liberation Front (ELF), the historic rival to the current governing party in Eritrea?

---

3 The "hierarchy of return" was discussed during a presentation for a workshop organised in the American University in Cairo (FMRS) on "Research on Refugees in Urban Settings: Methods and Ethics," April 11, 2003.

In aid agency reports there is no negative information about any "blond angel" cutting the water supply in order to convince reluctant refugees to leave. There is no voice of criticism. Also, I would add, there is a culture of secrecy and a lack of transparency that has led to such situations. Hiding these cases is now so commonplace that when an academic points out a human catastrophe it is impossible to admit honestly that a mistake was made or that the policy of blackmail was a total failure.

I agree with Antonius Robben (1984) that US "West Coast" sociologists such as Herbert Blumer, Harold Garfinkel, Erving Goffman, Aaron Cicourel and Harvey Sacks have inspired many scholars, ethnographers and historians, like myself, to focus on the dramaturgical dimension of the relationship between field workers and their informants. This dramaturgical aspect is not a theoretical framework lacking concrete verification. Here and again the works of Goffman (1959, 1963, 1968) remain highly pertinent for our understanding of the processes of interaction that develop in ethnographic encounters. "Ethnographers and interlocutors protect their public image and gain access to each other's back stage." (Robben, 1984) Um Gulsa camp was the backstage of the "blond angel" theatre and the title of this chapter suggests that the interaction between the "blond angel" and the refugee is the stuff of which drama is made.

In the interaction between researcher and informants, I had to manage, of course, my empathy for the victims and antipathy for "blond angels" in order to objectify my perception and cross the distance between emotion and academic description. I had to transcend the ethnographic anxiety (Devereux 1967:42-45) of a spectacle of suffering beyond ordinary suffering. Davis (1992) in his article "The anthropology of suffering" uses the metaphor of apocalypse to suggest suffering beyond ordinary or cataclysmic events.

The experience of Um Gulsa camp, an experience of extended privation due to lack of water in a hot climate, lasted from December 2001 until March 2002; a long agony initiated by a social organization that took a political decision to cut the water supply. This decision was the social product of an organization that did not take the decision by accident, but rather analyzed the situation and determined that cutting the water supply was an appropriate tool to provoke the departure of those thousands of Beni Amer who did not wish to repatriate.

Forced migrants and refugees are subjected to a radically more unbalanced relationship with the HO professionals who deal with them than other immigrants. During my research on African immigrants in Marseilles (Direche-Slimani and Le Houérou, 2002), I never observed the degree of vulnerability I saw with the Beni Amer in their interaction with others: whether host country, host society or aid workers. This vulnerability might be amplified and interpreted as a mark of singularity; that is, a marker of distinctive identity in the analysis of the forced migration situation. It is also a major argument for building a distinctive category, even though many scholars have argued that creation of this category could create a theoretical "*cul-de-sac*" (Bascom, 1998). Understanding their total vulnerability compared with other migrants is, however, not the only human evidence that demands a distinctive category: this vulnerability also creates psychological situations that present many singularities. One singularity is the special culture of the HO.

HOs possess a unique and homogeneous culture with its own jargon and myths. Their juridical vocabulary has imposed juridical categories such as "refugees," "irregular movers," "IDP" and "repatriation." These categories have shaped the study of forced migration. Academics should emancipate their analyses from these juridical tyrannies and avoid the context of the charity business. For a cultural anthropologist, and for a contemporary historian like myself, no institution or organisation should be above any cognitive process, or above any philosophical inquiry. The desert context is also part of the drama. This ethnography of everyday interaction between refugees and humanitarian actors takes place in the Sudanese desert, where water and food are so scarce and precious. In this circumstance, any staff person providing aid appears as an angel. When this angel cuts the water supply, the scene is then transformed into a nightmare for the refugees and the protective angel turns into the incarnation of evil. The context of casual "meetings" is key to understanding more accurately the unbalanced relations between HOs and their clients, and emphasizes the degree of pain that characterizes the interaction.

In the next section we will see how this interaction can have a dramatic impact, especially when refugees refuse to follow the repatriation programs set for them by UN agencies.

Those Who Cannot Return: Homeless and Hopeless in Sudan[4]

The Beni Amer nomads used to live in an area straddling the border between Ethiopia and Sudan (Nadel, 1945). They fled the war in Ethiopia and took refuge in Sudan. But now they find themselves in no man's land: no longer entitled to aid because they have lost their refugee status and unwelcome at home because they backed the "wrong side" in the war of independence. "They can go—they're no longer refugees," said an aid worker dismissively of Ethiopians

---

4 This section was also presented in an article for Le Monde Diplomatique (Le Houérou,

and Eritreans in Sudan, one of the world's poorest countries and currently host to 904,000 refugees.[5] The combined effects of drought and civil war, which resumed in 1983,[6] have sapped Sudan's fragile economy. The recent boom in oil prices has only partly benefited a country that is exhausted by crises and full of migrants, with foreign refugees as well as people displaced within Sudan. They are a huge problem for Sudan and for international aid organizations. Two-thirds of the refugees are concentrated in the East, in Kassala province, on the frontier between Sudan, Ethiopia, and Eritrea: 120,000 refugees live in camps[7] while 560,000 live outside, freely dispersed in and around urban areas. Eight out of ten are "Habasha" (Abyssinians), an old word for the inhabitants of the high plateaux of Ethiopia; but there are other forced migrants from Chad and Congo. The displaced persons come from the West (Darfur and Kordofan) and South of Sudan, which has been at war since 1983 (Prunier, 2002). The 1.8 million victims of the civil war (De Montclos, 2001) have flocked to the outskirts of Khartoum, Khartoum North and Omdurman. Displaced persons account for almost half of the population of Khartoum and its suburbs, and are the new beneficiaries of development programs set up by NGOs. Yet for the past two years the Sudanese authorities have been pressing the "Habasha" from Ethiopia and Eritrea to leave. International protection for refugees is governed by regulations. The Geneva Conventions stipulate that persons will lose their refugee status if the conditions that caused their initial flight disappear. The profound political change in Ethiopia in 1991, with the downfall of the dictator Mengistu Haile Mariam, justified the application of this provision, as did Eritrea's independence in 1993. As far as the United Nations is concerned, the "Habasha" are no longer refugees. After the overthrow of Mengistu, Sudan, Ethiopia and the UN High Commissioner for Refugees agreed to schedule the return of refugees. Toyota pickup trucks with loudspeakers drove around the districts with large Ethiopian populations promoting the benefits of repatriation, but the terrified refugees refused to sign up. In March 2001, the clumsy pressure exerted by UNHCR provoked a hunger strike in Khartoum. "Funding the journey home costs much less than feeding refugees for years. Refugees cost $130m in 10 years," explained a World Food Program official. "But we're not forcing anyone to leave. We're just stopping aid, that's all." That means ending weekly deliveries of flour, sugar, milk, and grain, and cutting off the water supply. It is a "clean-up or clear-out" policy to force those that have stayed behind to leave. The authorities shut down the camps and then they disinfect the area. In practice, the clean-up part of the policy has not been

---

6 See the preface by Alain Gresh in Le Soudan en question (Fawzy-Rossano, 2002).

7 These figures are reliable, as regular population censuses are conducted in the camps.

implemented, but international organizations have been quick to cut off the water supply. A disenchanted NGO head in Khartoum says:

> They are closing refugee camps and opening others for displaced persons. But sometimes they are side by side. Sometimes they actually occupy the same refurbished land. In Kassala, the UNHCR cut the water supply to a camp, but there were still several hundred people there who had refused repatriation and were determined to stay. A UNHCR official even asked to have the camp cleaned up. I replied that it wasn't our role and that we were a humanitarian organization.

There is no legal framework for the abandoned camps and their status-less occupants in the dusty desert of Northeast Sudan.

The old camp at Um Gulsa, near the Eritrean border, is typical. In December 2001 the UNHCR decided to close it, along with two others at Laffa and New Shagarab. The Sudanese say 8,000 people are slowly dying in the camps. The hospital staff have gone, the water pump has been dismantled and the school closed. There is an air of abandonment; the camp is a collection of shacks of scrap material. Several thousand Eritreans are holding out despite the lack of water, most belonging to the Beni Amer nomadic group. The founders of the Muslim League, the first party in Eritrea to demand independence, were Beni Amer. No reliable record has been kept of the numbers who have died since the camps closed in 2001. Asked why they do not want to move, the survivors reply: "Because we are Beni Amer, we do not want to leave." But the aid organizations refuse to make allowance for their origins. "If we start enforcing ethnic criteria, we'll never finish," they say. Their approach covers political situations associated with refugee status, but disregards the Beni Amer's unusual position. Yet 80 percent of the Kassala refugees are from Eritrea and two-thirds of those are Beni Amer, which means that their situation also has a political side. The tribe is largely supported by the Eritrean Liberation Front (ELF).[8] This relationship is confirmed by interviews in the camps: all the men say they belong to the ELF which was defeated by a rival group, the Eritrean Popular Liberation Front, currently in power in Asmara. As is so often the case, defeat has turned the members of an ethnic group into refugees and it is not clear how they will be able to rejoin Eritrean society. The people of Um Gulsa are not refugees, but they are social outcasts.

A UNHCR official in Asmara says: "Refugees are free to choose where they settle. They are not interned in Eritrea." He maintains that the real

---

8 The Eritrean Liberation Front (ELF) opened its first offices in Kassala in 1962.

problem concerns the cultural reintegration of people who have picked up Sudanese attitudes and habits. The refugees in the camps see things differently. It is hard for the Beni Amer to settle again, because their land has been confiscated and they are victims of segregation. Their successful reintegration is the most important political and social challenge facing President Isaias Afwerki's government in Eritrea. Afwerki is worried about the influence of Sudan and of Islamist groups on Beni Amer communities in the camps, where Islamist NGOs hostile to his government are supposedly at work. This complicates the prospects of the Beni Amer returning to Eritrea. But most of the people in the Um Gulsa camp are nomads, or women and children, with little interest in politics. They are not a traditional target for Islamists, who recruit mainly among the middle classes (shopkeepers and traders); it is only in comfortable camps, where there is plenty to eat, that attitudes are favorable to Islamists.

At Wadi Sherifa, a vast and well-organised camp, the market offers a range and quality of produce that rivals Khartoum.[9] Some of the shacks in Wadi Sherifa have parabolic TV antennas and the refugees tune in to the Al-Jazeera network. Many refugees here have well paid jobs. These two camps one impoverished and the other prosperous offer a striking contrast on the same semi-desert at the foot of the Kassala Mountains.

UNHCR has a $24m budget for the Eritrean refugee repatriation program; yet its overall budget for Eritrea is only $28m. The repatriation policy is a priority, and with reason. By the end of 2004 it aims to bring 160,000 people home. The UN gives each repatriate a five-acre plot of land and $200 to build a hut. UNHCR and the Eritrean Relief and Refugee Commission have convinced most of the Tigrinya Christians from the high plateau to leave Sudan; but support for the ELF by the Muslim Beni Amer from the lowlands makes it harder to justify across-the-board repatriation, even if community leaders have agreed to return to Eritrea. In Cairo in November 2001, a Beni Amer leader, who was one of the ELF's founding members, explained that he supported the repatriation policy. Exile in Sudan had deprived the tribe of its roots and status in Eritrean society. It was time for the Beni Amer to regain their former position in Eritrea, physically and politically. This, however, disregards the situation in the field and the concerns of people in the camps. To make matters worse the information campaign by aid organizations has been clumsy. The idea that they might soon be returning home has rekindled memories of the war between Ethiopia and Eritrea, and of famines. The older generation

---

9 Kassala province, well known for its market gardens, produces the best fruit in Sudan.

is reluctant to leave Sudan, though young people have flocked to sign up for the program.

UN repatriation experts have never taken such psychological factors into account. UNHCR argues the case for withdrawal of refugee status on rational grounds based on the political changes: the end of the dictatorship in Ethiopia and independence for Eritrea. Yet the populations at risk cannot forget their past, which stands in the way of plans for return. Many of the refugees we interviewed explained that they did not believe in the political changes that had supposedly occurred in their country. The information campaign to convince refugees to return home should have made allowance for their fears, however irrational. This would have overcome the stubborn refusal of the most defenceless refugees. Stripped of their refugee status, they watch powerless as the NGOs leave, crouching behind scraps of tarpaulin, often too thirsty to move. They repeat that the war between Ethiopia and Eritrea is not over, even though there has been a semblance of peace for two years. They are terrified to see UN Land Rovers invading their patch of desert. In March 2002, when a Japanese delegation came to assess the extent of the disaster before the dry season, the population of Um Gulsa did not react. The delegation organized a meeting of the elders on the site of the former hospital to hear their complaints. However the people in the camp could barely speak, numbed as they were by hunger, thirst, and sickness.

Now they are leaving it up to officials to settle their fate and decide who is entitled to humanitarian aid. The aid on offer is subject to strict conditions in line with defined priorities, legal rules, and administrative routine. In the name of law and order, theory is getting in the way of practical help. The Beni Amer who are Sudanese nationals qualify for aid and, as displaced persons, they may receive gifts; but the thousands of Beni Amer from what was once Ethiopia no longer count as refugees, despite their numbers. So, with a perfectly clear conscience, the aid organizations are shutting them out.

Dysfunctional aid is often influenced by a bureaucratic approach of the action that should be undertaken for the refugees. There is a desperate need to hear the voices of the refugees and to set up a more pragmatic action relying on long term appreciation and analysis of refugee situation from the inside.

Listening to the actors, putting the refugee at the centre of a heuristic process can be a positive approach. This methodology was experienced in the city of Khartoum and was relevant to study the strong problematic of history, historicity, and exile. The next chapter will explore the notion of loss of history related to displacement. Losing place can produce this symbolic cultural loss.

Chapter 5
Exile and Loss of History within the Ethiopian Diaspora in Sudan[1]

THE PRESENT CHAPTER EXPLORES the notion of histories in relation to urban exile among the Habasha communities (i.e., Ethiopians and Eritreans) of Khartoum. Forced migrations have radically displaced families and the resulting urban exiles have raised interesting questions concerning the conservation and construction of histories. With the disruption of the family unit, historical facts related to their roots have been placed at risk, potentially threatening the identity of these communities. Within a generation, memories will fade and a crucial repository of information related to the family heritage will be lost. This pattern is characteristic of any kind of migration, whether forced or voluntary in nature. In the case of forced displacement, the problem of historicity grows more acute, because being labelled a refugee or asylum seeker by aid agencies and other international institutional organs manages to limit the forced migrant's identity to a mere juridical concept. This paper aims to historicize the last wave of Ethiopian refugees in Sudan who came after 1991, supporters of Mengistu fleeing the current Tigrinya government. These groups have been in Sudan for more than 13 years, making it particularly interesting to question their respective relations to notions of history at large.

We explored questions related to historicity through an empirical exercise, a repatriation exercise conducted by UNHCR. At that time, tension

---

1 The theme of this chapter was explored during a field research partly conducted at Khartoum University with the collaboration of the Development Studies and Research Center. Sudanese University was more than welcoming and cooperative in that program and I want to thank them very warmly.

between UNHCR and the refugees was evident. While no urban refugee in Khartoum wanted to go back to Ethiopia, UNHCR was forcing refugees out of the country, arguing that political change in 1991 served as sufficient grounds to apply the cessation clause to the Ethiopian refugees. We questioned the refugees about their feelings toward repatriation. Among increasingly rational arguments, such as fears born of past political activities or an inability or unwillingness to break with newfound roots in Sudan, there was also evidence of deviant rationales for refusing to go back "home." Most interviewees did not believe that the changes that had occurred in their country were substantive in nature.

Figure 9: **Repatriation (Khartoum)**

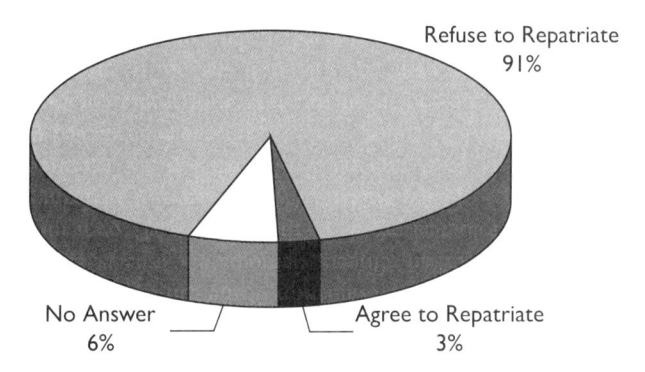

- Refuse to Repatriate 91%
- No Answer 6%
- Agree to Repatriate 3%

They denied that changes initiated by the new regime were for the benefit of the people; instead they emphasised the dismal belief that "things will never change." Consequently, interviewees tended to be wholly opposed to any repatriation activity conducted by the UNHCR and their government.

To use a euphemism, life for refugees in Sudan is not easy, particularly as material and non-material needs are far from being satisfied. Working with the Diaspora in Khartoum highlighted many points related to how a dramatic situation can destroy a community's "collection of souvenirs" and an accompanying sense of history, and how a stressful event can lead to a "pathology of memory" as studied by Bergson in *"Matière et mémoire"* (1939). The French philosopher explored alterations in memory witnessed after a particularly traumatic event. He demonstrated the existence of a pure personal memory related to emotional balance (Bergson, 1939: 191). The sociologist Maurice Halbwachs defended the collective essence of memory, countering Bergson that no memory is retained if one is isolated from a group or a community (Halbwachs, 1994:101). We used the insights of both

Bergson and Halbwachs as tools in analyzing and, finally, deconstructing the phenomenon of memory loss in this particular refugee context.

Figure 10: **Perception of UNHCR**

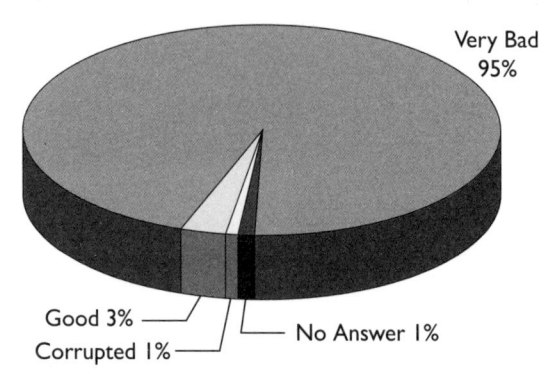

- Very Bad 95%
- Good 3%
- Corrupted 1%
- No Answer 1%

Is memory connected to the emotional balance of an individual, and therefore can it be challenged at any critical time? Or, instead, is memory only dependant on a given social context? What ramifications do the answers of these questions pose for the urban refugees of Sudan? How can one maintain memory in a difficult urban environment? What strategies do refugees use in rebuilding territories and preserving memories, if any at all?

Methodology

We interviewed 250 persons in Sudan in 2001 and 2002. The majority of interviewees were Ethiopian (90 percent), primarily Christian highlanders: Amhara from Shoa, Bagémder and Gojam, and Tigrinya from Tigré. In 1996, academic Gaim Kibreab observed that, among Eritreans, the Tigrinya ethnic group was most significantly represented in the Sudanese capital (Kibreab, 1996). Among Ethiopians, he considered the Amhara a majority with 90 percent from urban areas. For our field research, the majority of interviewees came from the major towns of the northern province (i.e., Adwa or Aksum).

The group of houses selected for this study were rented by people from northern Ethiopia, because a wave of refugees arrived from Tigre in Deim (a zone in Khartoum where a majority of Abyssinians lived) during that time.

Initial observations revealed several weaknesses and were thus considered as part of a work in progress. The research at hand was an attempt to conduct a microanalysis based on two ethnic groups (all Christians and all from urban backgrounds); we had no ambition to provide a general picture of a single community. The Abyssinian Diaspora is far from a coherent, homogenous group. The research effort concentrated on the Christian highlanders as researchers were familiar with their culture from previous research initiatives. Familiarity with the language facilitated investigations and approaches at large.

A questionnaire related to conceptions of time and cultural events was distributed to the refugees in the urban neighborhoods of Khartoum and in Cairo as well. We collected comparative data in both urban settings. The bulk of the questionnaire focused on historical events in the country. For example, we inquired about Adwa, a battle between Ethiopians and the Italian colonial army that took place in 1896. Adwa is the name of the major battlefield, but also the name of the capital of the Tigre Province in the North of Ethiopia. The battle is considered a significant historical marker in the Ethiopian highlanders' vision of history, and it is well known among all ethnic groups. The battle was used as a point of departure in asking interviewees to organize essays about this historical event. The relevant question asked was: What do you know about this battle?

Figure 11: **Adwa Historical Battle (Khartoum)**

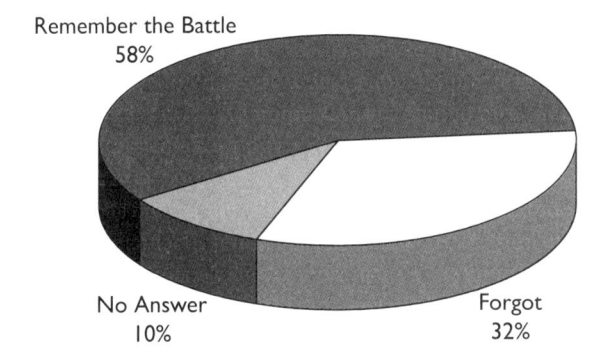

Remember the Battle 58%

No Answer 10%

Forgot 32%

The anthropologist John Beattie used this methodology in Uganda in the 1950s,[2] when he relied on a selection of testimonies from literate interviewees concerning culture. We tried to bypass the selection bias that is created when privileging a few individuals for enunciating their particular concept of culture. Thus, we opted to collect a larger pool of testimonies—from both literate and illiterate interviewees.

---

2 Beattie's experience was cited in Nicholas Thomas (1989). See Beattie (1965:30–34).

Interestingly, most Ethiopians took the exercise seriously rather than dismissing the research as "academically useless." Countless humanitarian actors have emphasised that in dealing with a vulnerable category of people, research is often considered an "intellectual luxury," underlining that people in need (e.g. refugees) were more likely to favor research that responded to immediate health and education needs. At times, questions surrounding the representation of time and history might be regarded with a certain degree of "amusement."

The Ethiopians' interest in the topic at hand was noted and appreciated. This group often considered it dignified to be dealing with questions of their history, rather than being consumed by immediate health and material needs. From here, one could also measure how cultural links might directly influence policies concerning the repatriation program.

Importantly, the subject of the research created no security concerns for the interviewees at the hands of the state security or other regulatory organs. This lack of concern allowed for freedom of expression and transparency throughout the research.

The research program was presented to Khartoum University, as we conducted interviews in neighborhoods where the Diaspora was most widely represented. In Khartoum we deliberately opted for the most visible concentration of Ethiopians, in the neighborhood of Deim. The market of this zone is a bustling meeting ground and center of human relations, providing a significant social reference for the Diaspora in this particular urban setting. No other locale in Khartoum is so central for the Ethiopians. We collaborated with a Congolese immigrant working in the *souk* (market) to find a suitable interview space that would put interviewees at ease. We asked people to assume false names in order to reassure them. At one point, our Congolese colleague was questioned by a security agent and we agreed to invite this agent to a meeting in order to protect the people of the *souk*.

Interviews were conducted in the *souk* in a space located between the aforementioned Congolese tailor and an Ethiopian tea seller. We worked in a visible, accessible manner in the public space, while also keeping the security informed as to our activities. The urban context in which we were operating is loaded with significance: born of interactions between the host society and newcomers: it defines a novel territory. There are about one hundred shops in the *souk*. Ten percent of those shops are rented by Ethiopians (tailors, hairdressers, tea-sellers, shoe cobblers, beauticians, spare parts shops, restaurants, etc). The hairdresser was a young, educated man who had been studying medicine in Sudan before being displaced. Both he and the tailor cooperated in the distribution of surveys, particularly aiding illiterate persons in filling out forms and translating essays on the battle of Adwa.

A significant number of Ethiopian women make a living by selling tea in the street. I spent hours sitting with such women throughout the research period. Little by little, news of the questionnaires spread. In the end, we collected three hundred responses. Of these, a hundred were not understandable in one way or another, and thus were discarded.

Misunderstandings surrounding my own presence were encountered, as many members of the exiled community assumed that I was assigned by the Canadian or Australian embassies to select the most literate persons for resettlement programs. I explained repeatedly, and it was also clearly indicated on the questionnaire, that the work being carried out was for academic and research purposes exclusively. The research assistants in the market were also crucial in this regard, explaining that we were interested in notions of exile and history. In addition, the essay on Adwa was at times perceived as an educational test—demonstrating the ever-present reference of resettlement in Western countries as an ideal, while also highlighting the fugitive mentality associated with transit. In order to prevent further misconceptions, I explained that I was not an agent from any embassy, nor was I associated with any resettlement program. Instead, the aim of my research was to understand the nature of their lives in Khartoum, and their notion of 'Ethiopianness' as related to historicity. Many expressed disbelief that I had travelled this distance simply in order to learn about their culture. "You came all the way to this dusty *souk* in this poor neighborhood to understand us?"

Some interviewees acknowledged that family ties were often lost or forgotten upon emigration. One Ethiopian told me of a brother living in a Western country who had asked him not to reveal his telephone number to the rest of his family who remained in Sudan. It seems that exile sometimes poses a challenge to traditional conceptions of African hospitality. Solidarity was often a forgotten value in the dusty Souk al-Deim. One interviewee, Mulu, explained to me that some who succeeded in getting resettled abandon their families, arguing that it was impossible to respond the many needs of the refugees left in Sudan. Indeed, sometimes a resettled man would forget his past, his friends and even his family in the "far south" of Sudan. Abraham agreed, arguing that the expectation that one would save one's family once resettled was potentially overwhelming. In the end, this group often felt abandoned—by their families, and particularly by the United Nations when asked to repatriate against their will.

It was in this difficult context that I attempted to convey the intentions behind the research. But this was not the first time I was forced to substantiate my intentions in carrying out research as a visibly "white woman" in a non-white context. In the difficult context of exile, refugees or forced migrants are deprived of any kind of historical density by "others." These "others" may be one's own government (you are considered an outsider) or an international institution, which reduces one's identity to "refugee" status—thus eliminating any recognition of cultural specificity and identity at large. In this context being poor translated into not having access to a history, and being locked into a merely juridical framework. Historical issues are "forbidden." An employee of the World Food Program in Sudan put it this way: "What do we care of that! History, ethnicity; we are here to feed people in an urgent situation and we don't play with such concepts."

Such a statement is perhaps emblematic of the de-historicizing tendency of humanitarian agencies. Historicity may be perceived as an act of defiance, especially in camps. Therefore the UN system, at times, consciously abolished differences in its dealings with the displaced. The creation of the word *refugee* was meant to be a universal legal solution. While it suited the immediate post-World War II context, history has progressed and the complexity of the current global refugee situation has challenged the legal architecture of the concept "refugee."

Such a notion is not new and has been deconstructed by academics such as Ahmed Karadawi, Barbara Harrell-Bond and, more recently, Liisa Malkki (1987). They consider the historicization of forced migrations and the international response as an intellectual challenge. But it is a tendency that is difficult to grasp among UN structures, which generally perceive migration as limited to legal frameworks. Thus, it is important to look at the refugee experience as a potential historical trace. Recording the timing of the migration period, recording the forced migrant's memories, and understanding his notion of time and the events remembered or forgotten related to exile are crucial endeavors.

The validation of this hypothesis regarding the importance of history was provided in Kassala as I interviewed Beni Amer who refused to return to Eritrea and lived in the context of a camp. They preferred to die in the desert (see the previous chapter and Le Houérou, 2003).

Presentation of Ethiopian Diaspora in Khartoum

The Eritrean population and their presence in Sudan have been widely studied by scholars, and much material is available on these subjects at the

Development Studies Research Center in Khartoum as well as at the Ahfad University of Women. Eritrean refugees have been studied at length by Gaim Kibreab (1996) and Tom Kuhlman (1990, 1994) from a socio-economic point of view. Incidentally, data collected ten years previously present many similarities to what we encountered.

The Commission Organization for Refugees in Sudan (COR) provides an annual record of the number of refugees in the country. As Barbara Harrell-Bond has observed in a seminar held at the American University in Cairo in February 2003, the statistics surrounding refugees have remained unchanged whether or not persons have been repatriated. In 2000, the statistics counted 217,280 Ethiopian and 544,379 Eritrean refugees in the country, while the total refugee population was 934,409. The total population of urban refugees in Khartoum in 2002 was estimated at 35,000 persons, 78 percent of whom are males.

We can recall the data provided by Gaim Kibreab (1996:132) about the evolution in Khartoum only:

Date	Number of Ethio-Eritrean Refugees in Khartoum
1974	300
1975	1,943
1976	6,116
1977	8,178
1978	6,238
1981	33,000
1984	40,000
1994	40,000

The significant majority of refugees in Khartoum are Habasha (Abyssinians). Congolese and Tchadians are not represented as strongly. As noted above, entire neighborhoods, such as Sahafa, Djeref, and Deim, are almost entirely populated by Ethio-Eritreans, while the majority remains Ethiopian. Such estimations are based upon conversations with interviewees rather than scientific calculations. Importantly, interviewees tend to overestimate the number of refugees, arguing that enormous waves of Ethiopians repatriated in 2000 had come back to Khartoum. It is difficult to quantify in this manner, though their estimate of Ethiopians (legal and illegal) in the Sudanese capital tended to be more than 50,000 people.

Studies about Urban Refugees in Khartoum

Few studies have been carried out dealing with African urban refugees. The majority of analyses have focused instead on rural areas. Gaim Kibreab has published a significant amount on Eritreans in Sudan, focusing on the impact of refugees on the environment and economy. Tom Kuhlman (1990, 1994) has also studied the results of a humanitarian mission in the Kassala region, exploring the economic impact of refugees in this eastern region of Sudan.

Kibreab's 1996 article in the *African Studies Review* provided an initial picture of the Eritrean and Ethiopian refugees in Khartoum. Kibreab interviewed 432 Ethiopian and Eritrean heads of household and used data given by COR-IC (Commission for the Refugees). Although such a general sociological presentation was a basis for my own approach, I was not willing to try to design another urban picture of those communities by presenting an evaluation or a counter-evaluation of the causes of flight, the difference between rural and urban refugees, demographic aspects, ethnic characteristics and the sociological profile of the refugees. My own information surrounding the age of the population was, in fact, not far from what Kibreab had described six years previously. Nevertheless, he interviewed Eritreans and Ethiopians in Khartoum, while I primarily interviewed two Ethiopian ethnic groups. In the end, his picture is far more representative of the whole community than my own. My intention was not to provide a general account, but rather to examine a specific aspect of the story of the urban Habasha refugees in Khartoum.

Reasons for Coming to Khartoum

Refugees in Khartoum are attracted for the typical reasons of job opportunities and the prospect of resettlement, but though these two causes are still to be observed, the primary cause of migration is to escape the current violence. This reason is particularly poignant when one is affiliated with the former regime. All interviewees were willing to be resettled in a Western country. Nevertheless, the transit period in Sudan is invariably a long one. Such transience provides countless obstacles to local integration. A transient mental state will also invariably influence what I will term a loss of history, or of a sense of historicity. Locked in a precarious limbo, refugees do not live in the present, but rather tend to project into the future.

Needless to say, it was difficult to hear the tale of a 77-year-old Ethiopian woman who had lived in Sudan for 44 years, begging to be interviewed "at once" because she was counting on the possibility of being resettled the following day: "You might not see me tomorrow because I will fly to America."

The difficulty of the situation is also a consequence of the policies of the Sudanese government. Importantly, an Eritrean sociologist inquired as to why millions of West Africans called Fallata in Sudan were never labelled as refugees, while suddenly, in 1967, Eritreans were labelled refugees (Kibreab, 1996). The reason is, at least partly, to be found in the historical response of international institutions to forced migrations (Harrell-Bond, 1986: 2-10). From the creation of UNRWA to the birth of the UNHCR in 1951, the international community has effectively constructed the concept of refugee. In addition, one must also account for the potential benefit that host countries garner from UN agencies.

During the Fallata migrations in the 18th century, no international law existed. As a consequence, the Fallata were never subjected to the juridical uncertainty born of contemporary transience. Instead, they perceived themselves as part of the landscape of Sudan. They were largely integrated into the fabric of the country. Nevertheless, the loss of historicity and the loss of historical references did not mean that one gained another historicity or identity. One may lose such reference points without appropriating particularly Sudanese histories.

On the surface (they are very often dressed like the Sudanese), the integration of the Ethiopians is often misleading. Cultural borrowing in such a manner is not necessarily proof of assimilation. For example, many Christian highlander women declared that wearing Sudanese traditional colored *thub* (dress) is in fact a means of being protected from harassment, as well as an effective means of avoiding the characteristic black Islamic '*abbaya* (cloak).

Habasha and the Representation of Time

Ethiopians and Eritreans constitute the largest and oldest group of forced migrants in Sudan. Their prevalence is well documented. The historical reasons for such prevalence are directly linked to the instability of those two countries, as wars and droughts have been common, sometimes occurring at the same time, over the last two centuries. Moving to Sudan because of external stress was, then, a very common solution among the people of the region, both before and after colonization. Nevertheless, quantitative evidence is not the only factor chosen for the study.

Pierre Bourdieu's theories (1993) on the dialectic relation between center and periphery have also been a point of reference. The French sociologist tried repeatedly to demonstrate that it was pertinent to question the periphery and the margins of a society in order to understand its center. He defended a micro-sociology based on everyday behavior to understand ordinary existence and was very much influenced by Goffman's approach. He wrote a homage to the Canadian sociologist as a "*decouvreur*" of what was so infinitively small.[3]

In other words, questioning marginalized groups was a pertinent entry point in the analysis of relevant political forces and rivalries in the region. For a contemporary historian of Ethiopia and Eritrea, this was a compelling hypothesis to explore further.

What can the refugees in Sudan tell us about contemporary Ethiopia and Eritrea? How can we extend our understanding of that part of the world by hearing refugees' stories? Why is this region one of the primary sources of global refugees after the 1960s?

Epistemology was also a primary interest. How could I examine a history of persons with a wholly different relation to time than that commonly known? In fact, most "academics" have been analyzing events in an ethnocentric manner. Their analyses have often been inspired by their cultural beliefs and their own representations of history read in the light of a theory of modernization. As pointed out by Francis Fukuyama, the imposition of Westernized standards stands as a universal truth (Fukuyama, 1992: 95). Such an ethnocentric manner in reading others' realities suggests a linear sense of history the conception of human history as a record of progress. From the Enlightenment philosophers onwards, the French revolution provided the strong belief that history will progress through the elimination of tyrants, and that authority will be based on a rational social contract (Rousseau) establishing all men as "free and equal in rights" (Fukuyama, 1992: 28). Fukuyama, like Le Goff (1992), underlines that we cannot observe any moral progress in the world's history. The progress of Science has not necessarily translated to an accompanying progress of conscience in this last century.

The history of the Habasha highlanders, unlike the Nuer (Evans-Pritchard, 1969:209), is also rooted in a linear basis. Time is understood in terms of a Christian (Coptic) calendar, while the religious representation of time starts with Adam and Eve and ends with the Last Judgement. Such a way of conceiving time may be completely different among other ethnic groups (Dassanetch, Afar, Saho, Maria), or the Hamitic and Cushitic groups. Dinka and Nuer from Southern Sudan once had an ecological sense of time based on cyclical seasons, marked by events such as droughts and rains (Evans-Pritchard, 1969:95).

---

3 Pierre Bourdieu, Le Monde, 4/12/1982. It was Bourdieu who introduced in France the theories of Goffman by arranging for the sociologist's main books to be published by the Editions de Minuit.

In accordance with the post-Durkheimian heritage, I agree with Maurice Halbwachs's notion that time is socially perceived and that memory is directly linked to a group's memory. No memory is isolated from a group (Halbwachs, 1997). The representation of time is inspired by the group, and thus remains collective. Given such a heritage, one can only approach a notion of time according to the groups under consideration.

The Calendar and Representations of Time

There is no universality surrounding the representation of time, even though modernization has imposed a standard calendar and a unique way of perceiving time. The prevalence of the Western clock has imposed a new age; even if the standard clock is far from one's cultural conception of time, one is more or less forced to adopt it in multiple contexts.

The importance of the calendar is then emphasised in this approach, not only because the calendar imposes a schedule of time but because it is directly born of religious patterns. It is difficult to deny that the representation of cyclical time in China is inspired directly by Buddhism, while the conception of time in the Arab world is based on a lunar calendar with years dated from the *hijra*.

Religious holidays are thus social constructs given the prevalent conceptions of time. *Al-Eid al-Kebir* (Great Bairam) is a direct means of asking people to remember the willingness of the Prophet Abraham to sacrifice his son, while it is also evidence that history is constructed by historians according to their perception and representation of change. In the end, history may be seen as a science of movement.

The Ethiopians' conception of time is based on Christian feasts. Whenever I made an appointment with refugees in Sudan, it was invariably in relation to the Sunday mass. Here there is a weekly rhythm and a linear perception of time. Thus, this group does possess a written history comparable to a European written history. In the end, the existence of old literature and a corpus of texts dealing about historical events in Ethiopia are of major importance in the formation of what we can term a historical conscience.

History and Kings in Highlanders' Traditions

Most of this corpus of texts is linked to political events. The first manuscript to be found was the *Story of Kings*, a book legitimatising the Solomonic dynasty. The history of the Amhara people focuses on the kings from the 13th to the 19th century. History became a tool for power and domination rather than a science; it was more a justification for existence of the ruling kings. Such a tradition has influenced the highlanders' vision of the world, as well as their cosmogony. The manner in which the past is organized is linked to this tradition, and history tends to be understood in terms of the reign of kings—comparable to the Middle Ages in Europe. Kings were, in fact, the main actors in history and people tend to refer to the past through references to a main actor: e.g., "It was during King Tewodros's government." Significant markers are the battles of kings, and Ethiopian history still privileges military events. History is the justification of the prince (De Certeau, 1975: 15), and one of these iconic dates within this history is the battle of Adwa.

Battlefields and Historical Memory

The battle of Adwa took place in 1896 and is still considered one of the most significant events in contemporary Ethiopian history. The battle was a victory of King Menelik over Italian invaders. Importantly, it was the first time a white army was defeated by a black one.

Symbolically the date is very important for the Ethiopian sense of nationhood. It is celebrated each year in all the corners of the country with huge festivities. It has been commemorated with mathematical regularity for more than a century and crosses ideological lines. The communist Mengistu, like the current Tigrinya administration, celebrated the anniversary of Adwa every year. Adwa is a national feast for the people of Ethiopia, much like the 14th of July for the French or Independence Day for the Americans: they all represent a fundamental marker in national history. All ethnic groups in the country have heard of this battle. Even if one seeks to, it is virtually impossible to ignore the anniversary, making Adwa a pertinent marker in measuring the representation of history among communities in exile.

Maintaining Memory in the Midst of a Loss of History

The repatriation of the refugee population in a city like Khartoum clearly appears on a map because the population is primarily concentrated in certain zones of the capital. Most of the neighborhoods mentioned above are "segregated zones." Here, the term segregation is used according to the definition given by the Chicago school. In the 1920s, Burgess (1925) was using census tracts (spatial units) in which different minorities represented more than 10 percent of the global population. While we do not have the luxury of such census tracts, rough observations indicate that in the vicinity of Souk al-Deim, the number of refugees or immigrants is more than 60 percent of the total population. My calculation is limited to the streets surrounding the market place. If we do not possess the instruments to call this spatial arrangement "segregation," we may use the concept of concentration of a Diaspora in a specific space. It has been enlightening to compare this with the social distribution of the Diaspora in another city like Cairo where the urban environment presents a completely different distribution of people. In the Egyptian capital, the community is dispersed, spread among many neighborhoods, thus making the residential strategy of the refugees totally different.

As far as Ethiopians in Khartoum are concerned, this concentration provides the community with a very rich social life. The marketplace of Deim was surrounded by many places of socialization. Restaurants and coffee shops concentrated in the *souk* were central in those spaces where refugees and Sudanese together shared games (dominos and cards). The Souk al-Deim presented many aspects of a capital for the exiled Habasha, providing a cultural space for the Ethiopians abroad. News and goods, whether material or non-material, were exchanged there. This platform for exchange served as a strategic point in observing urban networks in progress around the cafés or the tailor shops.

The group in Khartoum is, thus, geographically coherent, while in Cairo the community is increasingly dispersed. In Sudan, collective ceremonies were held in the vicinity. Weddings were organized on a large scale, and these and many other ceremonies facilitated connections amongst this community. Socializing was a common practice and spatially defined. In contrast, such bonds were not observed in Cairo, where social life appears to be weaker. Distances in Cairo are seen as a real barrier, or frontier, between persons, and there is a tendency to socialize in one's immediate vicinity. As a group living together, the memory is kept alive by continuous interaction with others.

Memory of Adwa

As indicated above, the choice of Adwa as a reference was not only inspired by the quantity of references about the battle in Ethiopian history, but also by artistic productions like paintings, theater, dance, music, etc. Amharic literature is fond of biographies of fighters, and the warrior is a traditional hero in Amhara culture. There are a remarkable number of biographies of courageous kings like Tewodros, who killed himself on the battlefield because he would not surrender to the British enemy.

Adwa is the victory of King Menelik—often considered the father of modern Ethiopia and the builder of modern Ethiopia. The battle is the symbol of ethnic unity under the imperial flag, and the mythology surrounding this battle is so iconic and crucial that is an apt point of reference in Ethiopian history.

I expected that asking questions about Adwa would be an easy exercise, a simple historical checkpoint. But responses from the ethnic group from Adwa, the town where the battle took place, proved particularly surprising. Results revealed that even Ethiopians from Adwa did not know very much about the battle. Among the approximately one hundred people who had attended formal schooling, 32 percent had not heard of the battle; 58 percent of interviewed persons were able to tell us roughly what Adwa was about, while 10 percent did not answer the question. Among the 32 percent who claimed to know nothing of the battle, 20 percent mentioned that they used to know of it, but had since forgotten the details.

According to the research at hand, duration of exile did not influence memory or the concept of the nation's past. Some interviewees, who had been living in Sudan for more than 40 years could remember histories very accurately, whether the Adwa battle or other key historical events. Duration of exile, however, caused a loss of knowledge of history when it was combined with social isolation. A bonded group in exile is more likely to preserve historical knowledge than an isolated individual. Cultural bonds have been fundamental in preserving memory.

In Cairo, we observed that the immensity of the town created a form of retreat into oneself and social isolation that had important consequences in the process of the loss of history. Within this urban context, 70 percent of the refugees reported that they had forgotten Adwa. In addition, one of the main points revealed by the research was that social isolation provoked depression among the refugees in question. Immense stress was then a real challenge in the protection of cultural heritage. The two different urban settings resulted in very different relations to history at large. This question at hand was irrelevant to Eritreans, as the history of the Eritrean nation is a wholly different one; Adwa does not belong to the pantheon of Eritrean events.

In both Khartoum and Cairo, the duration of exile influenced integration in local society. In addition, the processes of local integration were also related to the loss of collective memory surrounding the history of the Ethiopian nation.

Kibreab's data on the age of household heads found that most were young (1996:151), but in our data, among 100 persons, 60 were older than 45 years. This difference can also be accounted for by the characteristics of the neighborhood in which the research was carried out. As my Sudanese colleagues have related, Deim was historically the oldest Ethiopian space in the town; one might meet refugee families there who had arrived in Khartoum in the late 1960s, or earlier. The oldest person interviewed in Khartoum was the 77-year-old lady mentioned earlier, the Tigrinian lady waiting to be resettled in America. Here, even after an exile of 30 years or more, persons are still mentally in a transient state. This particular woman resisted being rooted in Sudan, even after so many years.

Figure 12: **Repatriation (Khartoum)**

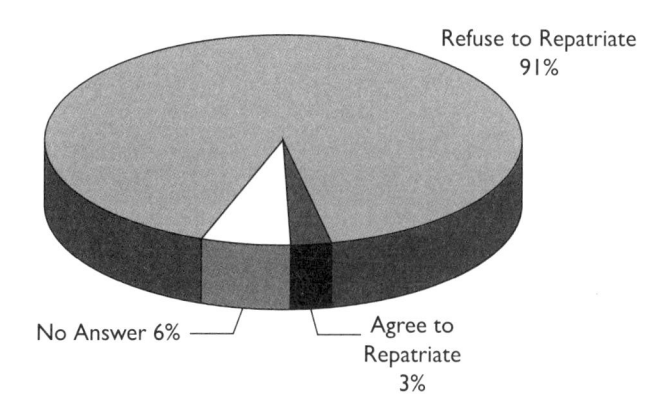

- Refuse to Repatriate 91%
- No Answer 6%
- Agree to Repatriate 3%

Most interviewees were supporters of the Mengistu regime, and were still considered refugees because they did not fall under the cessation clause. Most of them were over forty years old and had had important responsibilities in the Mengistu administration. An entire class of middle class administrators excluded from state institutions was obliged to escape. In many interviews, interviewees declared their admiration for the past dictator and expressed nostalgia for the Mengistu period. As part of a social group supporting the Dergue's policy, such people were recognised as refugees by UNHCR as non-post-1991 migrants. Interviewing this group showed how deeply the Mengistu regime was rooted in the Ethiopian social context. Contrary to what is commonly stipulated, the dictator had followers from many different origins, including Eritreans supporting the idea of Ethiopia and Eritrea as one nation. These were primarily nationalists defending the "*etiopyia ticdem*" (Ethiopia forward!) concept of "Greater Ethiopia," a manifestation of the king's notion of a nation—uniting diverse ethnic groups behind one flag and a pro-Amharic culture.

The interviewees were rarely critical of the Mengistu regime, despite the fact that it was one of the bloodiest regimes in the horn of Africa. The dictator has been referred to as "the Pol-Pot" of the horn of Africa, in reference to the huge displacements and resettlements that took place during his rule—ultimately resulting in thousands of deaths. In fact, in countless situations, interviewees expressed admiration for the dictator. At one wedding, an Eritrean *azmari* (singer) spontaneously composed an apologia about Mengistu. This particular group lived with a political nostalgia of the Mengistu era.

The duration of exile is much longer in Khartoum than in Cairo, primarily because it is easier to leave Egypt. There are many opportunities in Cairo that one cannot find in Khartoum, where people tend to become bogged down for ages. Yet, even if exile is longer in Khartoum, we were surprised to compare the results of the enquiry with the urban context of Cairo.

The loss of memory was most acute in Cairo. Most interviewees in Cairo had deserted mandatory army conscription, were under significant psychological stress and were often in constant fear of deportation. Such panic was one of the primary causes of depression and social isolation, which, again, seems directly linked to what I have termed a loss of history and memory.

Figure 13: **Adwa Historical Battle (Cairo)**

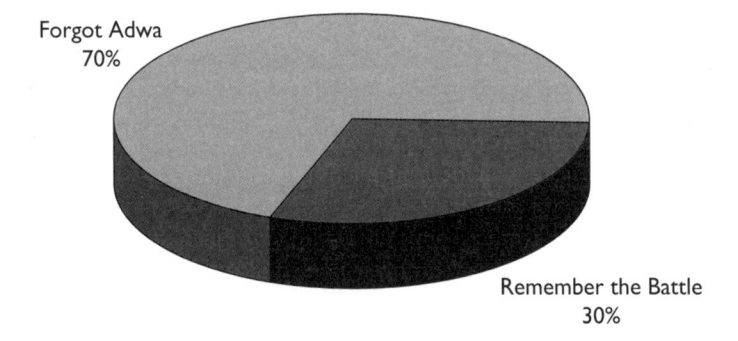

Forgot Adwa
70%

Remember the Battle
30%

These last observations thus give the philosopher Bergson the last word when he stipulates that a particular shock may result in a "pathology of memory" Bergson, 1988). Here, the French philosopher's observations are a useful analytical tool in understanding the relationship between trauma and memory and collective histories. Often, at the origin of a forced migration event is a drama (individual or collective) that has effectively pushed people from their countries of origin. Such a "push factor" has a heavy psychological impact. While the representation of time and history admittedly will vary from one group to another, suffering abnormal pain has a noticeable effect on the process of loss or preservation memory. There is an urgent need for further academic research in order to measure the consequences of political violence on the subject of historicity, as manifested here in the particular case of the Abyssinian experience.

Being focused on everyday effort, living the present time, and forgetting about the past are the strategies adopted by the most vulnerable portion of the refugee population (female heads of household). Remembering the lost country is seen as a luxury when they are faced with everyday burdens. We will observe in the next chapter how everyday violence can be the dominant aspect of Sudanese refugees' experience in Cairo, for instance in their relations with the Egyptian population also displaced from Upper Egypt. We will study two displacements: Dinka refugees from South Sudan and *sa'idi* farmers migrating to Cairo in one of the most vulnerable neighborhoods on the edge of the desert.

Chapter 6
Violence or Avoidance Strategies in Arba'a wa-Nus[1]

THIS CHAPTER IS BASED on field research conducted in Cairo in an informal area (*'ashwa'iya*) called Arba'a wa-Nus, which means "four and a half" in Arabic.[2] In the current work, we explore the everyday interactions between Sudanese refugees and Egyptian society in one of Cairo's poorest neighborhoods. We emphasize the notion of proximity ("vicinity") as a pertinent analytical tool to study casual relationships between hosts and their guests. From this perspective, our project aims to throw light on everyday life and meeting strategies, avoidance or conflict strategies of actors in their day-to-day transactions, as well as to study the networks of those transactions on a micro level in a specific location. In short, we try to explore social proximity and distance within a limited spatial sphere. Our project was to give an interpretation of the impact of the morphologies of cities on the integration process of forced migrants into host society.

Violence or Avoidance Strategies in Arba'a wa-Nus

Arba'a wa-Nus is an area exactly halfway between Madinat Nasser and Suez road. It was constructed without any regulation or government authority; the area is, therefore, characterized as informal. As noted by Galila al-Kadi (1987), the land was seized by a businessman, Esmat al-Sadat, who took 500

---

1 Based on a paper submitted at the workshop organized by Fabienne Le Houérou at CEDEJ on 24 April 2004: "Diaspora in Cairo, transit territory and transit position."
2 It is four and a half kilometers from the Suez road.

hectares and developed a housing estate called "Ard al-Haganna." It represents a new form of urbanization that first appeared in the 1970s in Arab cities. These informal settlements co-exist with formal settlements and are characterized by existing outside the rules of national legislation. Sometimes these urban areas spring up on lands where it was forbidden to build (e.g., Arba'a wa-Nus) or, in other cases, the construction does not conform to legislation. The French geographer Pierre Signoles et al (1999:22) emphasized the multiplicity of designations of these areas as "illegal," "informal," "spontaneous" or "anarchical" and opted for a more neutral term like "unruled settlements" or "contested settlements," a definition used by Omar Razzaz for the city of Amman (Razzaz, 1993).

Today, most apartments in Arba'a wa-Nus have electricity; but not everywhere is there running water and what there is is often polluted. Streets are unpaved and garbage lies uncollected in the middle of the main road. Most buildings are very rough, often left unfinished and usually without a coat of paint. Sudanese families use newspapers to cover their walls and to protect themselves from humidity. Arba'a wa-Nus has no police station and all administrative offices are located down the hill in Madinat Nasser. At the border of this neighborhood, all forms of transportation are readily available with many micro-buses heading directly downtown. Arba'a wa-Nus cannot be considered a "no man's land:" the zone is tightly linked with Madinat Nasser and exists with the support of that district's infrastructure. Nor can Arba'a wa-Nus be described as an original exercise because the area is comparable to other zones of spontaneous settlements, such as Dar al-Salam (Hopkins, Mehanna, and al-Haggar, 2001).

Comparing different ethnic groups in the same town allows us to identify common elements in the urban dynamics of integration. What are the shared experiences among those different Diasporas in a megalopolis such as Cairo? Why can we not find Ethiopians or Somalis in Arba'a wa-Nus? Does the fear of "otherness" or the fear of "others" form a common bond linking forced migrants? For example, the anxiety expressed by the Ethiopian and Eritrean communities is not comparable to what we have observed in Sudanese communities. We cannot defend the hypothesis that fears among the Sudanese due to their illegal presence in Egypt do not exist, rather, the fears are similar but are expressed in different ways. When many Ethiopians chose to hide in their apartments, Southern Sudanese faced up to Egyptian society, despite their precarious legal position. That is to say, the Sudanese continuously interacted with others in the streets and reacted very openly to "otherness."

Permanent invention has a collective expression for the Dinka people in the Arba'a wa-Nus area. More than fear, the forced migrants there demonstrate a predisposition very quickly to erupt violently or antagonistically based on their avoidance strategy. All the evidence indicates that the main characteristic of life in Arbaʻa wa-Nus is of violent relations expressed daily in all kinds of relationships. Interactions between Dinka women and their men are violent. Interactions between the Dinka and Egyptians are violent. Children, as well, show brutality when playing or communicating with each other. Relations among Christians are violent; relations between Christians and Muslims are violent. Violence is the bond linking the inhabitants of Arbaʻa wa-Nus.

Street Violence in Arbaʻa wa-Nus

Contrary to what has been said for so many years, the Sudanese Diaspora is very sparse in Arbaʻa wa-Nus. Satellite photos show us with mathematical precision that the population of the informal zone is not more than 35,000 people, as registered by the survey in 1995. The Sudanese Diaspora is concentrated on the top of the Hamza hill, near their church and school. The Sudanese display a residential strategy of living in groups for security reasons. With the high degree of urban violence in the neighborhood, as noted above, the Sudanese say candidly that they choose to stay together in order to defend themselves collectively in case of attack.

In the few streets occupied by the Sudanese community, many groups have conducted surveys to register families for schooling and food aid; thus there is no mystery concerning their number. We are talking about 300 Sudanese families originally from Dinka areas, and more precisely from Awil in Bahr al-Ghazal. Ninety five percent of my informants were originally from Awil. Around Cairo, even in the universities, rumours suggest that there are 500,000 Sudanese in Arbaʻa wa-Nus. When you compare that urban myth with reality, the discrepancy is rather remarkable. How did this significant divergence from the truth come about?

On the one hand, it seems that scholars or journalists who took quick strolls through the area came back under the illusion that there were thousands of families because of the residential concentration of those families in a few streets. In addition, Egyptians feel they have been invaded because Sudanese families, in their desire to live together, occupy whole buildings. This Egyptian unease consequently leads to an exaggeration of the number of Sudanese.

Exaggerations arise from fear. The fear of invasion is first expressed through exaggerated numbers that provide a dramatic dimension. European countries experience similar fears and are prone to similar overestimations. In our research in Egypt, we found that the myth of numbers is even believed by the refugees' neighbors who blame them for a number of very specific hardships. In interviews, many Egyptian families argued that rents had become very expensive since the arrival of the Sudanese.

> *Two years ago, to rent living space for the family cost us only 50 pounds; now the rent is 75 pounds because of the Sudanese. The prices of rice, oil, bread, sugar, and flour also rose because of the Sudanese.*

When asked why the Sudanese, rather than the economic crisis of the Egyptian currency, was more likely to be the root cause of impoverishment in the neighborhood, people responded:

> *When you are poor sharing a small cake, getting any of the cake becomes more difficult. It is like this for housing. Getting a house is difficult; finding a job becomes impossible. So we are poorer. We have no example where the dispossessed improve together.*

But others noted that the Sudanese are clients and "consumers" and, in that sense, they promote Egyptian employment. A baker in Arba'a wa-Nus commented that the Sudanese were his main clients and that he was grateful to them for giving him a job. Many shopkeepers shared this commonsense opinion of the Sudanese as clients who bring income and jobs to the local market.

Two other sentiments concerning the Sudanese presence in Egypt and its influence on the local economy were also expressed in Arba'a wa-Nus. First, many Egyptian families believe they now have light in Arba'a wa-Nus because the zone had became so crowded that the government had recognized the necessity of providing electricity. The coming of electricity was thus seen as a manifestation of legality and the sign of a process of formalizing the existence of this area. Two years ago when I first visited the neighborhood there was no light. Opinions that the local infrastructures have either improved or worsened because of the Sudanese are polar views that coexist with no nuance, or "grey" area, in between.

Public space is where violence breaks out on a regular basis. Streets are the main theater for this violence. Many quarrels between the Sudanese and Egyptians start as a result of disputes between children. Seemingly every day, children fight with other children; their childhood scraps in turn drive the parents into conflicts. I filmed a Dinka mother ready to beat up a young Egyptian Coptic teen. As I was filming, several neighbors and bystanders intervened to calm her.

Conflict explodes at all corners during the daytime and involves women as much as children; but the situation becomes more dangerous when men are involved. Many gangs exist in Arba'a wa-Nus, and they draw in the numerous unemployed young men. Sudanese men have reported being attacked in the street with razors. The conflict usually starts with a verbal insult that degenerates into stone throwing and ends with razor or knife cuts. Observations reveal that this daily violence is not based on religious discrimination. There are some 10,000 Copts in the zone, particularly around the Coptic church located near Sudanese Center and school. Conflicts arise between Coptic Egyptians and Catholic Sudanese. Sudanese also oppose Sudanese: Sudanese gangs have used razors against other Sudanese.

A simple ethnic or religious interpretation of violence would thus be erroneous. Poverty is the main enemy of daily life in Arba'a wa-Nus. Precise data for aggressions and manifestations of aggressiveness in social relations demonstrate that everyone is affected by violent interactions. No one escapes the daily brutality. We observed a small girl "torturing" a dog. As she played with a stick, she hurt the animal very badly. Even animals, it seems, do not avoid casual cruelty in Arba'a wa-Nus. Hitting, hurting, cutting, and wounding are part of the physical conditions of life in the area. This violence is not restricted to the Sudanese; instead, it is a whole context of displacement and uprooting.

The reasons behind the violence are not solely due to the level of poverty that people endure. Research on livelihoods would prove that Arba'a wa-Nus is no worse off than the Dar al-Salam or Ard al-Liwa districts in terms of harsh economic conditions. So what could explain the prevalence of violence in Arba'a wa-Nus?

I would propose a social hypothesis about an original confrontation of two displacements that face one other. Most of the Egyptian Copts who share the same spaces as the Sudanese and gather in the same streets come from Upper Egypt, and in particular from three governorates: Giza, Minya, and Sohag. These Copts, although still in their own country, can be considered as forced migrants seeking economic relief. Of the people I interviewed from Minya, all without exception were escaping poverty in their villages. Their main goal was to find a house in the densely populated Arba'a wa-Nus.

Forced Migrants from Upper Egypt

During a lecture given at CEDEJ on 22 October 2002, Ayman Zohry, an Egyptian demographer, presented his research about the unskilled temporary labor migration from Upper Egypt to Cairo (Zohry, 2002). He noted that the Upper Egyptians living in Cairo were compelled to come to the metropolis; due to the absence of any alternative they are, in theory, forced migrants. Job opportunities and sometimes simply the availability of houses formed the push-pull factors behind their exodus from Upper Egypt.

In my field research, men originally from Minya explained that they came to Arba'a wa-Nus in order to find a roof for their families. Often they spoke of a cousin, a brother, or some other family member who had already moved to Cairo and who was settled in Arba'a wa-Nus. These relatives reported that life was better in Cairo than in their hometown, and encouraged other family members to come with assurances of the support in Cairo provided by the church with its assistance programs for the dispossessed. In many cases, informants did not actually come in search of employment; that is, theirs was not a labor migration as we might call it. Instead, the informants said they sought to escape poverty, to escape the absence of land and to find simple shelter for their families. In addition, informants more often attributed their move to Arba'a wa-Nus to a broken shelter or a family conflict than to a search for jobs. In our view, many situations recounted by the interviewees were more comparable to a "fugitive" situation than a constructed (i.e., planned) migration project for a better life.

Yet, even in this degraded environment, most informants from Minya expressed satisfaction with their housing conditions and standards of life in Arba'a wa-Nus. They stated it was still an improvement over what they had in Upper Egypt. Houses were portrayed as luxurious in comparison to those available in Upper Egypt. For the most part, interviewees were fleeing a total lack of material support at home.

A 41-year-old informant, who was an unemployed and unskilled laborer, declared that he considered his life a "happy one" because he had a roof and a television: things that he could only obtain by coming to this neighborhood. When we seemed surprised by this statement, he said he would never go back to Minya and added: "You do not know how it is over there!" He was originally from a very poor Coptic family with eight brothers and sisters, and he was running away from family conflicts. He could not rely on family solidarity in Minya. This, he explained, was why he had no alternative but to migrate to Arba'a wa-Nus.

Historically, the Upper Egyptian movement first took place during the British administration. Zohry considered post-modernization migration as an ambitious one because motivations were high (better education and better life as a whole). This selective migration was followed by mass migrations during Gamal Abdel-Nasser's industrialization of the country, when thousands of unskilled workers were attracted by job opportunities in the new factories (Zohry, 2002). In the 1970s, with Anwar al-Sadat's open-door economic policy, another migration from Upper Egypt ventured northwards because of the building boom in the Egyptian capital. During this period two major satellite cities were built: the 6th of October City to the west and 10th of Ramadan City to the northeast.

In Zohry's typology there are three profiles of forced migrants from Upper Egypt, which more or less correspond to the historical parenthesis mentioned above. First are the *old migrants* who are integrated into the city. Next are the *established migrants* who kept their Upper Egyptian identities and settled in degraded areas. Lastly, a third group is comprised of the *circular migrants* who live in Cairo but regularly return to their home villages.

The Coptic men interviewed in Arba'a wa-Nus differed slightly from Zohry's profiles. Most informants said they were not willing to return to their home villages although they were very careful not to lose their "*sa'idi*" identity. I am tempted to consider this group of men as belonging to a "broken migration:" migrants who fled disaster situations, broke the rules, and are in a general situation of rupture (or borderline situation). In this sense, the group interviewed in Arba'a wa-Nus were much more desperate than the average migrants from Upper Egypt. Although it is difficult to measure social vulnerability, we may consider the Coptic group interviewed in Arba'a wa-Nus as a wave of Christian outlaws seeking shelter rather than opportunity; and so, in this regard we should not view them as "opportunists."

Even though many informants were "outlaws" from their family and breaking the rules, they still paradoxically followed a family pattern in their movements. In Arba'a wa-Nus, a close family member would prepare a place for the newcomer and try to reconstruct whole families on a spatial basis. Also, a forced migrant in Arba'a wa-Nus feels more secure within his family's entourage, because, as they consider it, a man is less vulnerable when he is among kin. This strongly held belief motivates migrants to attract other family members by telling them how good life is in Arba'a wa-Nus. In particular, the possibility of obtaining a cheap house is a well-shared strategy to attract kin. As family members progressively occupy the space, a man's social isolation ends and a sense of security is created. In addition, an individual's importance is related to the size of his family, its cohesion and its spatial organization. These factors can all be enhanced by bringing more kin to the city. Social life is based on family activities, and prominent families rule the area. For example, when there was a problem at a Sudanese school, the church adopted a strategy of meeting the heads of families in order to discuss the matter. This technique served to solve the problem to a certain degree. After discussions with family elders, the Sudanese school was not attacked for many months. Justice in the neighborhood is organised on this familial basis. Matters are discussed among families. It is extremely rare that problems are raised outside the social network of clans in the close vicinity of the site.

Dinka Displacement in Arbaʻa wa-Nus

In addition to the "*saʻidi*" displacement and spatial concentration based on kinship, there are the South Sudanese refugees who experience another kind of displacement in Cairo. The Sudanese base their residential strategies on an ethnic pattern. They tend to gather in the same area according to their ethnic affinities. There are 300 South Sudanese families living in Arbaʻa wa-Nus. As mentioned above, most are Dinka and the people I interviewed were all from the same town in Bahr al-Ghazal. In Arbaʻa wa-Nus, the Dinka, Nuer, Shilluk and Barya easily share apartments together, but you would very rarely have found a westerner from Darfur before the crisis in this region in 2003-2004. The Nilotic tribes, also, consider they have numerous cultural affinities. The only Nuer I interviewed said his culture was similar to the Dinka culture. This very common opinion can be found in the very early British anthropological literature concerning Sudanese Nilotics.

Another similarity between the Sudanese and the *saʻidis* is that their residential pattern corresponds to person-to-person information transmitted by telephone. Generally, refugees arrive at Ramses railway station and go directly to Arbaʻa wa-Nus. Sometimes they stop in the church of the Comboni mission in the Sakkakini district. Informants explain that they select places like Arbaʻa wa-Nus because the rents are the cheapest in the megalopolis of Cairo. Like the *saʻidis*, finding a house for the family is the major concern. In the end, the residential strategy relies on the socially motivated free choice to live with one's ethnic group where, as noted previously, one feels more secure. Social investment, therefore, follows a logical choice based on vicinity that tends to give privileged solidarity to the immediate proximity. In essence, the closer spatially an individual is to ethnic and birthplace companions, the closer he gets to a family's solidarity set. In many cases, as informants put it, life would have proved impossible for the Dinka Diaspora without this keen sense of ethnic solidarity. Father Claudio, from the Comboni church in Sakkakini, pointed out that Sudanese have a very sharp consciousness of solidarity.

The Dinka are a product of a strict egalitarian upbringing and, like the Nuer, their political system is deeply democratic. Seventy years after Evans-Pritchard's studies, we observed that even now the sense of democracy remains alive. Much evidence shows that the Dinka are also easily roused to violence in the streets of Arba'a wa-Nus, as they were in the past in their traditional environment. In addition, we should not forget the precise portraits made by Leinhardt (1961) and Evans-Pritchard (1969) about the political systems and many other common points between the Nuer and Dinka tribes related to their economy and cosmogony.

> His turbulent spirit finds any restraint irksome and no man recognizes a superior. Wealth makes no difference. A man with many cattle is envied, but not treated differently from a man with few cattle. Birth makes no difference. They strut about like lords of the earth, which indeed, they consider themselves to be. There is no master and no servant in their society, but only equals who regard themselves as God's noblest creation. (Evans-Pritchard, 1969:181)

This equalitarian education and attitude creates a deep form of solidarity. In Arba'a wa-Nus, we observed neighbors (who were not kin but who shared apartments) assisting each other. In the absence of any family links, mutual assistance is very vivid on the scale of the entourage. If one individual has a surplus, it is immediately shared with others (Evans-Pritchard, 1969:183). It is a duty to share in Arba'a wa-Nus and selfishness is severely judged and can be a case of social rejection. On many occasions, we directly observed the reality of these traditional reactions. Sometimes they "beg from another with equal persistence" (Evans-Pritchard, 1969:183). Very often Dinka women asked me to give my earrings to them or asked for my watch; so we regularly went to Khan al-Khalili to buy jewellery. It was always shared in a very democratic way. It could become the object of quarrels and sometimes shouting during the distribution, but after the negotiations everyone seemed satisfied.

From observations made during five months of field research we must recognize that the solidarity described by the early British anthropologists remains a strong reality in exile. Nevertheless, as we will see, this solidarity possesses its limits and its own boundaries. In a city like Cairo we observed varied forms of solidarity according to the different African communities. The process of transit in Cairo has transformed the ways people interact in their own communities. Thus, comparing different ethnic attitudes towards solidarity is very heuristic.

The experience of displacement in Arba'a wa-Nus has not destroyed the solidarity network, and every social organization of the Dinka in Arba'a wa-Nus shows a high sense of ethnic solidarity. On the other hand, the Upper Egyptian experience demonstrates the same kind of result. Families prove to be as tightly connected in Arba'a wa-Nus as in the countryside. A lot of duties are exercised collectively, including accompanying a pregnant woman to the hospital or taking care of a baby during the hospitalization of the mother. The sharing of burdens is very common.

I recall a personal experience in Arba'a wa-Nus. Just as we were about to start our interviews with our main informants, we found a wounded man bleeding in the Coptic church. The man was drunk and claimed that he had been beaten up by six Egyptians. He went to the church in order to protect himself. The man was not from Arba'a wa-Nus. He fell unconscious so we decided to take him to the hospital. He was too heavy for me to support alone, so we asked people in the streets of Arba'a wa-Nus and then in Madinat Nasser to help us. Everyone refused except the *sa'idi* daily unskilled workers of Zone 10, who stopped work to help me carry the wounded man. Ten in number, and without a word, they very effectively helped the man. It was a metaphorical answer to my question about solidarity in Upper Egypt. The two displacements have this value in common, a value that was never destroyed by the poor conditions of life in Arba'a wa-Nus, and flourishes despite its daily brutality.

Giving and Giving Back

In a context of urbanization in an informal area created by forced migrants with no economic growth, gifts and counter gifts replace the mediation of money: gifts tend to be transformed into payments. Not giving back what you have received from another can be viewed as an act of aggression. The circulation of objects is also combined with a circulation of attitudes. Babysitting, cooking, and teaching are part of the multiplicity of actions that can be understood as an exchange of currency. In an environment where money hardly exists, helping your neighbor is a form of payment. Paying back your neighbor can take many different forms. Creativity in this exchange is very obvious. Any aid, help, or support that might have value will be counted and exchanged, all based on the value of cows. Evans-Pritchard wrote (1969:16), "*cherchez la vache*,"[3] and you will find the Nuer. In this situation, you will also find the Dinka. Even in the informal area of Arba'a wa-Nus people count their benefits in terms of cows. During this field research, I witnessed that even in the absence of cows (many informants had actually never possessed a cow), cattle remain in the abstract the highest valued item and the "gold exchange standard" in the mind of the Dinka people I interviewed.

---

3 In French in the original.

The gift is never the fruit of a free action. Nothing is more calculated than a gift. That is perhaps one of the reasons why the wounded man mentioned above was not helped in Arba'a wa-Nus, when we tried to carry him along the neighborhood's streets. When I asked why no Dinka in the neighborhood helped me, they all answered that it was mainly because he was from Ain Shams, another district of Cairo. He did not belong to the place. He was out of place, and belonged to another net of solidarities in another neighborhood. The man was not from the place and, thus, was not worthy of help. In any case, he would never return the help he received. Solidarity has a spatial logic and is not a concept above context. It is shaped by space and social representations. Because of the geographical distance of Ain Shams, the man was left on the ground.

"He is not from here!" The expression of the man as an outsider was unanimous among all my informants, and they all found it strange that I would ask for further explanation. It was obvious that there was no social obligation to a man they did not know, even if he belonged to the same tribe. This categorical statement was very similar to putting boundaries to solidarity and insisting on the spatial limits of the gifts. These boundaries were so obvious that it was the kind of evidence that Harold Garfinkel would very much value in the social fabric of everyday life. By creating a territory, refugees and migrants have also delimited it with boundaries.

Is that territory an informal territory or a spontaneous territory? A segregated zone or a no man's land? These are the questions geographers and urban researchers ask regarding the great megalopolis of Cairo. Where are the limits of informality when most of the city's population has no access to legalized housing? Where does it start and where does it end? Is the case of Arba'a wa-Nus one of the aspects of the total urbanization process taking place in Egypt? The question can be posed from the perspective of property and ownership and the laws of Egypt, but it can also be studied in the symbolization of cultural exclusion. The space translates the social segregation of the city in a materialistic way. Space is filled with sense and is full of sense.

Arba'a wa-Nus is not a shanty town, except around its margins and in very specific places. Buildings are constructed of bricks and are similar to buildings in other informal areas of Cairo such as Dar al-Salaam. Housing is poor, but cannot be compared to the anarchical aggregations of hovels found in certain suburbs in African capitals.

New residents of Arba'a wa-Nus from Upper Egypt or Sudan are producing their own sense and creating their own representations. They use new images and new words aggregated with ancient words to determinate the place. Arba'a wa-Nus is called "Taba," "Hamza," "Haganna" or "Ezba" according to different social groups. The territory does not exist as a concrete and recognized object. It is not an empirical fact. The territory is the product of a process of symbolisation that cuts and demolishes all materialistic aspects.

The wounded man was an instructive example of that process of symbolization. Community ties are always dominant and determine behavior. The community of the living overrides differentiation based on descent. Territorial relations are thus based on a community basis. Territory is shaped by the people who occupy it and the space gives us the most striking and spectacular illustration of that symbolization. The hill of Arba'a wa-Nus is demarcated at its front face by a line of pink, Venetian-style buildings that actually delimit the legal area from the informal one. These new buildings are a clear manifestation of petty bourgeois style and particular taste. They border Arba'a wa-Nus like a pink ribbon. A ribbon of sense separating two worlds: the forced migrants (Upper Egyptians or Sudanese) and the middle class population of Madinat Nasser. Even though there is no legal title to the land the apartments for sale are luxurious, showing the permanent creativity of "property developers" and estate agents. The people attracted by these products are young, middle-class couples who cannot afford to buy an apartment in Madinat Nasser: lawyers, doctors, and junior officers are the new owners of these apartments. From the back windows of their apartments they can see, behind wrought iron bars, the *favellas* (slums) of Arba'a wa-Nus. Their front terraces and balconies have a view onto Madinat Nasser. These buildings are like social barriers that separate two different worlds. Their message is that, in the end, law concerning land is never a handicap for the "connected people" (i.e., the working middle class) who can still reap benefit on a borderline.

Comparing the Dinka refugees in the Egyptian capital and their interaction with the host society with another Sudanese ethnic group is a fruitful approach. It gives us the sense of what is universal or singular about exiled communities and south to south migrations. Movement from black Africa to the Middle East; refugees from Darfur arriving in mass to escape the current atrocities in their country—Egypt is Sudan's main door for escaping traumatic events.

The last chapter will explore the dynamics of Fur refugees in Cairo and their daily relations with Egyptian society.

Chapter 7
Ordinary Contacts between Refugees from Darfur and Egyptian Society

THIS CHAPTER IS BASED on fieldwork in Cairo among exiled communities of refugees from Darfur. These refugees claimed to be stigmatized because of the color of their skin. What is it to be a survivor of ethnic violence today in Cairo? How do people negotiate their daily life? We will explore these questions in this chapter. We will here and again use the cinematographic methodology, using scenes as an analytic tool to explore every day life occurrences and the multiplicity of contacts.

Scene One

Aisha is a refugee in Cairo; she is from Jebel Marra in the center of the house of the Fur (Dar-Fur). She arrived in Cairo in 2002 and now she rules a kind of restaurant where all clients are refugees from Darfur. Her Egyptian neighbor is knocking at the door of her cafeteria in a very rough basement with no natural light: a meeting point for the Fur community in Cairo. The scene starts at 8 a.m.

> *The Egyptian neighbor:* "Hello! Hello!"

> *The researcher talking to Aisha:* "Does he call you "Chocolata" like the others?"

Aisha: "No, with him it is not the same. He is here every day with us!"

Mohammad (the Egyptian neighbor): "Sudan and Egypt are the same country!"

The researcher: "Are you originally from Upper Egypt?"

Mohammad: "Yes my father is from Asyut!"

The researcher: "Do you know what is going on in Sudan?"

Mohammad: "Yes, there is a civil war. All the newspapers are talking about it but I do not know the details of their war…"

The researcher: "Do you come here every day?"

Mohammad: "Yes, but I do not know their culture! Anyway I have never asked any questions about their culture. I come here as friend to drink tea and I'm not particularly interested in their traditions! It is not my business! I come to share good moments with them and to chat about everything and nothing! That's it!

The researcher: "Aren't you interested in these traditions?"

Mohammad: "The Sudanese interest me as good and gentle neighbors, like polite and enjoyable people! I am interested to talk about our common interests but I do not know Sudan, so I do not share Sudan with them! Sudan! Darfur! This is not my reality! To decide who is going to clean our common balcony and veranda this is my concern!"

Aisha: "Solidarity is what we have in common!"

Mohammad: "We are brothers and we help each others! For example the Sudanese go to bed very late at night, everybody knows that! They play cards and dominos until two o'clock in the morning. Consequently the morning after they find it hard to wake up! I know that, so in the morning I come and knock at the door and I wake them up! I am a morning clock for them! A life clock! (laughing) Every morning I sing "Esha! Esha! I am the '*messaharati*'[1] of the Sudanese!"

Analyzing the Context

The scene was recorded in its totality because it a very pertinent window for studying the relations of neighborhood and interactions between "aliens" and "natives." It shows new types of relations at work between these new immigrants and Egyptian society. This transcription would be hazardous and rather senseless without exploring the immediate context. We are in a rather wealthy neighborhood not far from Soliman Gohar Street. This avenue is very much under the influence of daily migration from the rural periphery of Cairo and the centre of the city. There is a daily market in Soliman Gohar Street where peasants arrive with their horses and wagons, setting up at 5 o'clock in the morning. With its concentration of cafés, the street is the theater of a multiplicity of meetings and everyday contacts between a population of forced migrants and refugees from East Africa and peasants from the Nile Valley, who are daily migrants.

This road was very close to where I used to live in Cairo; the market was then the place where I used to do my shopping but also my fieldwork; it was my living place, a strategic point of human observation at a micro level for very ordinary situations.

Daily meeting was a methodology that I adopted because it gave a sense of continuity and normality on a repeated timing between "them" (the refugees) and the "others" (the Egyptians). A schedule of well-programmed interviews could not give the same level of reality. Concretely it was at the heart of my direct intimacy and in my ordinary relations where I was present at the same time as an actor and as an observer of the multiplicity of relations between forced migrants and their hosts. Being a stranger, a French citizen, lent my position an easier point of view. I was the tool of a kind of reflexivity for the movements of strangers in their interrelations. Every day I shifted from the level of everyday shopping to a scientific observation. In the field frontiers were never clear; I was meeting the refugees every day in the food market. Sometimes while doing my shopping people from the exiled community from the horn of Africa (Ethiopians, Eritreans, Djiboutians,

---

1 The messaharati is the person in charge of waking up the believers for a last meal before fasting during the month of Ramadan.

Sudanese) that I used to run across, knowing that I was collaborating in the legal aid program created by Barbara Harrell-Bond, would ask me to assist them in preparing their files to present their cases favorably to the UNHCR. In this context I was recognised as a collaborator of the FMRS program. My nomadic situation was also a factor for abolishing frontiers even if I was in a comfortable status as an academic; being a stranger was to a certain point like a distinctive biographical essence (Appadurai, 2000). At the ethnographic level there was a community of experience linked with a certain circulation and nomadic habits. Even if the movement of the refugees was a forced movement and my mobility a chosen destiny, as outsiders we had a common bond.

In this context I am the neighbor of Aisha and Mohammad. Mohammad is an immediate neighbor. He is employed by a local yogurt manufacturer and at 8 a.m. he is the first one in the building. He starts his day's work with the first activities: cleaning the common space shared with Aisha.

Between Mohammad and Aisha a relationship exists during the working hours from the morning until the late afternoon. The contacts do not go beyond the working experience. These exchanges are punctuated all day long by gatherings like the one described above in Scene 1. These contacts are repetitive and automatic and most of the time silent: Mohammad can come and take his tea with Aisha three or four times a day, hardly speaking. The subjects treated are the cost of sugar, tea, milk, and the food items related to their business. Political events or international news are never discussed or even mentioned. Even the Darfur crisis, which all Egyptian media were discussing at that time in May 2004, was never a subject of discussion or exchange of views. Darfur was never on the day's agenda. The contact exists at the junction of their shared experience when their two realities intersect.

My instrumentalist view is corroborated by the testimony of Mohammad when he asserts: "Darfur is not my reality, to the contrary knowing who will clean the common space today is my concern."

They are united by a set of interests: Aisha and Mohammad wish the veranda to be clean for their clients. The contacts exist on a utilitarian level and at the same time also go beyond the addition of interests. The element of pleasure is part of the contact: drinking tea several times a day is a major extension of limited good relations between neighbors. Mohammad puts it this way: "Gentle neighbors, enjoyable and polite people."

The above skills have an explanatory value. Mohammad drinks tea at Aisha's place because he enjoys her company. The adjective "gentle" is very commonly employed by Egyptians to characterize the Sudanese. What can be understood as "gentle" is, in reality, the concept of *adab* (good manners).

Adab is a way to be in society; it defines acceptable social behavior. *Adab* is measured and appreciated in a social context; it is a question of dignity. The concept has many significations in history and Islamic dictionaries have a multiplicity of definitions. *Adab* is not an individual characteristic but is essentially situating a person within a group. To be polite with others, to control your way of speaking to others in all circumstances, is more or less, in the occidental culture, related to self-control.

This sense given to *adab* is not far from what Anita Fabos has defined in her PhD thesis (Fabos, 1999:2) as a characteristic of hospitality, generosity, reciprocity, and dignity generated as an ethnic resistance to Egyptian hegemony but also giving a certain space for similarities.

The meaning given today by scholars is not related to the genesis of the concept and its ancient definitions. The *Encyclopaedia of Islam* introduces the idea of *adab* as being synonymous with *sunna,* "habits, hereditary norm of conduct, tradition" received by the ancestors or other characters that we can take as models (like s*unna* was for the Prophet and his community). The concept is evaluative according to history, and means "good quality of soul," good education, urbanity as an equivalent of courtesy. At the beginning of the Abbasid period *adab* was more or less equivalent to the Latin concept of *urbanitas.*

I have observed in different contexts that the *adab* is also a form of sophisticated courtesy. This quality was often attributed to the Sudanese by Egyptians. The latter often expressed the idea that the Sudanese were polite (compared with the Egyptians). A sort of social refinement was attributed to the Sudanese in their relations with "others;" marks of respect were demonstrated by a series of gestures and manners linked with being "well educated."

Offering tea at any hour of the day is one marker of this "upbringing;" it is more like a ritual in Sudan. Many researchers refer to the way they were welcomed in Sudan with hospitable manners. What we learn from Scene One is that the concept of *adab* is not only related to the Arabs or Arabized populations of Sudan but also extends to African populations like the Fur, the Zaghawa, and the Masalit. Cultural identification through Islam has largely penetrated the non-Arab populations. The *adab* concept equally has a very high moral value among non-Arab tribes. Aisha is not Arab, she does not declare herself as an Arab, she claims an African identity: she is a Fur from Djebel Marra, her Arabic is very rough. She belongs to a well-known Sufi order *(tariqa)* in Darfur. Mohammad sees in Aisha the essence of gentleness and politeness. This fundamental element is crossed with other sources, different interviews of the African communities in exile in Cairo, victims of

Forced Migrants and Host Societies in Egypt and Sudan

the current conflict in Darfur, opposing "cultural Arabs to Africans." The notion of *adab* belongs to their codes and social norms. Therefore they express their adherence to a moral value deriving from religious belonging.

When Mohammad expresses the idea that Egypt and Sudan form one country ("*balad wahed*"), he stresses a stereotype of a Sudan being only a prolongation of Egypt: a natural continuum. This is a popular stereotype in Egypt largely shared by the population.

This field research also proved that the stereotype was as well represented in academic as in ordinary circles. It is an historical reference to the past of the two countries. A common history has linked the two countries, as we all remember that Sudan was "Anglo-Egyptian." The British influence was quite brief and was rapidly diluted in the passage of time while the Egyptian impact was much more subtle and durable.

The British condominium was established on 19 January 1899 after the army of the Mahdists was defeated. In reality, at this time the real tutor was the British administration. They were the actors of the administrative re-organization of Sudan. The British imposed their rules in the South through a few officers acting like local majesties, and under the influence of Christian missionaries motivated to seek the Christianization of the populations of the South.

The Umma party was traditionally a political cadre for the *Ansar* heritage and identified as pro-Egyptian. One of its historical leaders, Sadig al-Mahdi, great-grand child of the Mahdi himself, evoked his Egyptian ancestors when we interviewed him on October 28, 2004. Egyptians were largely mixed with the Northerners of Sudan. One of our informants declared that perhaps 10 percent of Northerners had Egyptian ancestors. A real ethnic mixture proved to be very influential for the future relations between the two countries. Family links kept on working like a political factor of unity.

MacMichael (1967), using the testimonies of the Arab geographers, reflects in his studies on the Berber origins of the Upper Egypt population and the invasions of Sudan during the 18th century. Let us remember that the Hawwara tribe did really dominate Upper Egypt and Northern Sudan in the 18th century. In Sudan, they were represented by two distinctive groups: the Hawawir nomads from Dongola and the Gellaba Hawwara in Kordofan and Darfur.

These elements of information are very rough and caricatured but they tend to demonstrate the reciprocity of influence between African and Arab cultures. For the Egyptians, Sudanese are *sa'idis*, a little darker than the Egyptian *sa'idis*. Between the south of Egypt and Sudan there is a geographical proximity that can be translated into cultural proximity.

Popular stereotypes fabricate a sort of amalgam; and the popular language expressly refers to the notion of "*balad wahed,*" which is a kind of illustration of the process. The Sudanese is a real neighbor for the Egyptian.

Scene Two

The second scene takes place in Aisha's cafeteria in Dokki, a meeting place for all the community of Fur, Massalit, and Zhagawa, the three populations which have been the victims of the horrors committed by the Janjaweed—a militia recruited among Arabic-speaking nomadic tribes in Sudan. Most militia members belong to the Baggara set of tribes, as Sadig al-Mahdi mentioned in an interview in Cairo[2]

> *The Janjaweed are mainly recruited through the Baggara and Jaymailiya; they are mainly camel owners, populations with an Arab pedigree but who have constantly mixed with other tribes by intermarriage for centuries.*

The Reizeigat, Misseeiria, Humur, and Hawarzama from Kordofan are also identified as Baggara. They can be found in Chad as well.

Aisha is speaking again. She is in her kitchen preparing a traditional dish, the " *'asida."*

> *I'm waiting for only one thing: to go back to my country! I do not like Cairo! I can't stand it! I don't like the cars! Noise! Always noise! Cairo is like an endless path to nowhere! In the Jebel Marra it was very green. I had a lot of trees. Nature is beautiful in my country! Green, it was green! Here I have lost the sense of taste! The taste of our fruits were delightful and the smell of our trees in flower! How do you want me to like the Arabs! They hate us, us the blacks, they hate us! That's it! It's very simple!*
>
> *Very often I feel like a cockroach in their eyes! My clients are most often Fur from Darfur. Every day when they come to my cafeteria they are attacked by the Egyptians. They beat them. Every day they are insulted. Here in my place we are among exiled people and we feel security in being together; but as soon as we go out we hear insults. The dominant insult is "chocolate" but there is also "Bango-*

---

2 Interview by Fabienne Le Houérou, Cairo 28 October 2004. See: http//archquo.nouvelobs.com /cgi/articles ?ad=/20050202.obs

bango." We are beaten every day, so of course I dream about Jebel Marra. I dream to be in the summer at the door of the mosque with my grandfather.

The Context

It was very early in the morning and Aisha found her cafeteria in complete chaos and disorder. The night before young refugees from the Fur community had played dominos and cards all night long, leaving the cafeteria in a very awful way. She showed evident signs of tiredness and disappointment. She was collecting the "rubbish" left by the young men (glasses, cigarettes, leftover food). Her voice was very nostalgic and sad. A very important number of refugees I met during my fieldwork traced their sorrow back to their land and their families. Often families and land were mixed in the "Image/Souvenir." Refugees listed the names of their trees to insist on what was most precious in their eyes. I have mainly heard Fur farmers and I have observed an extreme "attachment" to the products of the county. A fruit from the earth is not a metaphoric figure but a powerful image. All the time during our interviews Aisha never ceased to remember the perfume of her lost home. It is a very ordinary theme in refugee academic literature in the field of forced migrations. In a different context Lisa Anteby, during her research on the Fallasha who had migrated from Ethiopia to Israel, noted the powerful relation between exiles and the items imported from "home" (Anteby, 2004). The importance of the codes of food sharing is a very strategic point of identity construction in exile. Being outside home tends to put the migrants in a process of over-estimation of every imported food (like coffee for the Ethiopians).

"Here" and "there" are combined in a ritualized commensality used as a marker of identity. Bjorn Curley demonstrates in his academic research (2002) how collectively drinking *aragi* in Cairo was a powerful metaphor of Sudanese identity. The drinking ritual could fabricate social inclusion or exclusion. In Cairo we observed that exiled communities were capable of any kind of sacrifice to get "food" from home. In Khartoum II, in front of the Ethiopian church, there was a traditional market where you could find *awazé* (hot sauce), *berbéré* (hot pepper), and cultural clothing for men and women. Ethnic markets are not only to be found in an occidental megalopolis, they are also present in different societies of the South. These markets have the same community roles as they have in our modern cities (Paris, London, New York) for diasporic populations because they have a communitarian function (Raulin, 2000).

The past in Darfur is imagined like a patchwork of smells. These essences bring us back to the rural world of farmers and to the village economy. For Aisha and other refugees nostalgia is related to the seasons: the harvest time, the games of children in the rivers. An idealistic world completely opposed to a gigantic city like Cairo. The density of the urban population in the Egyptian capital is seen as a threat and a risk for farmers used to a peaceful environment with no highways and few cars. Cairo is perceived as a scary giant capable of devouring migrants. "I do not like Cairo, noise, always noise!"

A survey from 1983 made in Sudan states that there were six million people in the whole of Darfur (a region almost as big as France). The refugees find the city excessively populated (16 million inhabitants) and polluted, and get sick of it when they first arrive. The circulation of cars is incessant and the nostalgia for rural sounds is combined with the rejection of the noise of Cairo.

Violence Committed against the Refugees

The notion of "the Arabs" is like a miscellaneous category. Aisha mixes together Egyptians and Sudanese nomads. All are identified as "Arabs." As a short cut connected with the violence Aisha was submitted to, she is simplifying "Arab" identity and drawing a kind of caricature; the process of denomination is essentially a response to being identified as a black woman. Caricatures answer each other. Therefore when Aisha uses the term "Arab" she actually suggests "lighter" as opposed to "darker." The racist insults the Sudanese experienced in Egypt in public places, openly, constitute a fundamental experience linking the Arabs from "here" (Egypt) to the Arabs from "there" (Sudan).

In Sudan, in Darfur, as in Egypt, she feels the *eyes looking at her* stigmatizing her (Goffman, 1963). She expresses the wound (produced by a stigmatizing outlook) with this very powerful expression: "Very often I feel like a cockroach in their eyes." The stigmatizing outlook provokes the feeling of losing dignity. The cockroach is a repulsive "thing" and as a housewife Aisha judges the cockroach as the worst "thing" on earth. She fights them in her cafeteria because she finds them "disgusting." When Aisha gives the cockroach as a symbol of racism it has a multiplicity of meanings in her Weltanschauung:[3] "It is dirty, moving at night, black, and reproduces rapidly."

---

3 Kant (1984) uses this concept to express the infinite intuition of the world situated as a world and not as chaos. This conception of the world is more or less a vision of what the world could be for the subject who lives in the world, an intuition of the meaning of the world or a personal conception of the world.

Everything is there. The stigmatizing representation is complete. It gathers all the stereotypes used by racists for the "Black" in Egypt.

From Aisha's point of view there is a destiny of hatred based on the slight difference of skin color: darker/lighter. All evidences demonstrate that lighter is conceived to be superior. This symbolic violence is represented like a destiny. "Cockroach here (Egypt) and cockroach there (Sudan)" stresses the extreme vulnerability of these refugees who live in a frightening world in Cairo.

Ordinary statements about "color" put in perspective the emergence of what we can call an archetype (in Jung's theory) regarding the contacts between *Black* and *White* (even if there is no real *Black* and no real *White*. Everybody is Black in this Sudanese desert). In expressing this common sense about lighter-skinned people hating darker people, Aisha and other women interviewed give a form of historical destiny explaining this incompatibility.

"There is nothing we can do; they hate us so we can't like them." Despise is a real barrier which does not allow a meeting point. The disqualifying process acts like an insurmountable wall.

Observing, questioning, and analyzing the process of disqualification in the exiles' community, the actors gave a repeated assertion of the perception of slavery. When interviews went deeper the refugees found themselves talking about the ancient wound of being slaves and slave-hunters in the past. The Baggara were the specialists over the last three centuries in organizing hunting programs—especially in Darfur in cooperation with the sultanate.

The humiliating past of slavery when the "Blacks" were captured by Arab tribes is not very far away in a country which was well-known for selling human beings. We should not forget that the caravans of Darfur and the slave trade were organized by the Bedouin Mughariba tribe and remain very acute in people's memories. The road of the Darb al-Arba'in (the forty days' route) appears like a door between Egypt and Sudan for the slavery trade. The merchants were active before the 18th century, and the first mention of the sale of slaves was dated to 1573 (Walz 1978).

Asyut in Upper Egypt was a famous market for Sudanese trade in the 19th century. Slavery represented 39 percent of imports, with 46 percent of the slaves imported from Darfur. The historian Terence Walz (1978) stated that in the 18th century, "Darfur was Egypt's chief supplier for black slaves."

The stigmatizing outlook and the ridicule are related most of the time to a very distant past of total alienation and a fear rooted in the representation of Arabs as predators. Beyond all these fears we find the fundamental experience of the hunter and his "prey."

I will consider the fears and the ridicule as a spiral of stereotypes out of their historical context. Old roles have been revitalized and are pushing towards frozen attitudes. French anthropologists discussed long ago the emptiness of the concept of "ethnicity," demonstrating that the colonial administration was at the genesis of the construction of ethnicity. It is also pertinent for Sudan and the British: "divide and rule" norms constructed the difference between Southern and Northern Sudan. While we can ask ourselves the pertinence of the categories of Black or Arab in Sudan, what makes more sense is to understand what the actors intend by the categories. Sadig al-Mahdi explained in an interview in Cairo the notion of Arab identity, which is, in its essence, a statement that a lot of Northern Sudanese share:

> You see the Arab identity is cultural! All Arab identities are cultural! Even here in Egypt the Arab identity is cultural! You see, if you want to know the ancestors of the Arabs they will tell you it is Ismail. But he is a Jew! His mother was a non-Arab Egyptian! It is only his wife who comes from South Arabia. Anyway Arabs are very clear about their cultural identity. It is the culture that makes sense, not the race! In effect the Prophet himself said, "Being an Arab is not a question of father or mother; anyone who speaks Arabic as a mother tongue is an Arab!" So Mohammad gave to the concept of "being an Arab or not," or Arabism, a cultural definition. You will find in Sudanese tribes like the Rezeigat that have very black skins and who think about themselves as Arabs because of this cultural definition. You can find in Sudan other tribes with clear skin that do not see themselves as Arab.

Anthropologists give another view of what is cultural: the language is not the main point but culture, as stated by Jean-Loup Amselle (1990), is more like series of "critiques," conflicts, or peaceful habits used by social actors to negotiate, continuously, their identity. Nothing is really fixed but is in constant movement and flux, as demonstrated in Appadurai's (1996) academic research in cultural anthropology. The concept of "Arabism" developed by Sadig al-Mahdi is very limited.

The ancestors of the Fur were Arabs, like the founders of Kordofan and the Waday kingdom (Ibn al-Tounsy, 1851).

The fiction of the origins can turn into a war machine and an exclusion process. Origins are produced by communities' imaginations. Collective mythical stories become true for the people. The reality of the myth transforms the imagined story of origins into a true identity. The powerful energy of imagination is to transform any lie into a truth. Fiction is then nourished by reality and so on. All film-makers have experienced the very fragile frontier between the two. Imagination can be a circulation of dreams (Appadurai 1996) but also its contrary, as it can prove to be a rigid repetition of frozen habits.

As we saw in Chapter Four regarding blond angels (aid workers) and refugees, the need for myths is a human necessity to generate the strength to continue to live. Communities in exile have proved to be very attached to their myths. Myths are not true or false on the level of imagined community (Appadurai, 1996).

The stereotypes of what is an Arab or what is a Black African collapse completely at a micro-level of everyday experience. Daily interactions prove to be—in this fieldwork—the only way to change the representation of otherness. The method used for observation stresses the theatrical relations between humans. Scene One at the beginning of the chapter evokes the conditions where Aisha meets Mohammad in the context of neighboring contacts with the Egyptian society. Using video to observe these interactions underlines the minimal characteristic of every day contacts. People meet each other through details, not during philosophical discussions. Even if Mohammad knows the problem in Darfur he never mentions it. Their shared experience is their common interest: "*Who is going to clean the common space?*" is a key question for them. Reality is open to details in their infinite littleness in the heart of ordinary life. Aisha declared that Mohammad was not like others (she means other Arabs) and the young Egyptian man maintained that Aisha was a decent and gentle lady generalizing that "all Sudanese are gentle."

Studying micro-meetings underlines the frequency of reactions of singularizing the one who was met. Somebody you have really met is always *different (*from the ignored one that you have never encountered and who remains unknown*)*. This world made by a myriad of small contacts offers us a sociology in continuous construction and tends to prove that racism is a form of dead representation disconnected from the fluidity of life. This frozen representation of others can be dissolved in the energy of life. Shared experiences produce new forms of sociability that have to be invented, as Aisha and Mohammad did.

Scene Two is stressing with acute intensity the internalization of the stigma (Goffman, 1963) through ordinary sight. Aisha is discovering in Cairo that she is assimilated to a horrid insect (cockroach). The racist glance is associated with insults and attacks like a progressive violence erupting from perception to aggression. The escalation is paradigmatic to ordinary explosion of violence in Cairo. In that case Arba'a wa-Nus is very similar to what we observed in another site like Dokki or Maadi. Observation in different zones demonstrates that the site is of course an influential factor but should not be overestimated.

Aisha swallowed the indignity of the way she was seen. Her place is symbolically assigned (cockroach) in the urban setting. The difference is then expressed through a mark that functions like a stigma (being black); the color of the skin is a distinctive marker and a determinant element of understanding a person. These signs are observable in everyday life and in small things.

Emphasizing the infinite littleness of daily interactions was certainly Goffman's most inspiring approach for filming the scene. Focusing on self (persons) is the task of most film directors and the method of the Canadian sociologist is very much heuristic in building a filmed ethnography.

Eliot Freidson stated, during the Goffman memorial session in 1983, that his work was valuable and durable because of the humanity of his style (Freidson, 1983). Bourdieu expressed the same judgment about how passionately the academic observed realities with a particular intuition on details. (Bourdieu, 1982). Little things which constitutes, in the end, a real order.

In the study of forced migrations this observation based on little things should be an open door to encourage more ethnographies on "small objects," like the one written by Bjorn Curley (2002) studying Sudanese displacement through the symbolic "thing" of Aragi.

Chapter 8
Conclusion

CUTTING ONESELF OFF FROM reality or becoming overly aggressive are the two extreme responses given by populations on the move. Ethiopians, Eritreans, Somalis, Sudanese, or East African communities, in general, see Cairo as a transit point before following their stepwise migrations that will take them into another world (Le Houérou, 2004). Going to the West is the shared goal of these forced migrants from the Horn of Africa. Their dream of being resettled is so strong that it gives UNHCR a key position in Cairo (and elsewhere, of course). As stated by an UNHCR document, Cairo currently shelters one of the largest urban refugee caseloads in the world. For the majority of these refugees, the Egyptian capital has a limited transit function and role in an itinerary that will take them to the West. This essence as a place of transit is, thus, extremely important to understanding the process of integration into the host society and the social organization of communities on the move.

Their social organization is very much influenced by the precarious status of being a "nomad"—an urban nomad—who plans his or her life in Cairo and Khartoum (for the Abyssinian refugees) as a provisional stop before proceeding to further migrations.

This transient essence was a pertinent tool of analysis in cities like Cairo and Khartoum. The consequences of the transit mentality, as seen in Chapter II, are extremely complex and invade the totality of a person's life. When forced migrants are not resettled, but forced to stay (against their will) for a long term, it creates a lot of difficulties and a set of desperate social situations.

In Khartoum, as I mentioned in Chapter Five, I related the case of a 77-year-old lady who told me, "Please interview me today because tomorrow I will be in America." The lady was a Christian Amhara who had spent 35 years of her life in exile in Khartoum. For all these years, she always thought "tomorrow" would bring resettlement. Actually, the lady had been rejected by UNHCR but needed to tell herself a fairy tale because she disliked her miserable life in Khartoum and dreamt of another; she had to lie to herself to find the strength to survive her desolate environment.

A researcher in the early 1990s (Kuhlman, 1990, 1994) warned that resettlement programs were harmful to refugees because they created a fiction that would never be realized. In my field research, I confirmed that the transit period tends to be extended and that the sojourn proves lengthy in Khartoum for the Abyssinians. Sometimes, the entire life of the refugee is spent under the "umbrella" of that transit mentality and "*Weltanschauung.*" Even though agencies were very clear on the chances of resettlement, the refugees themselves need to create fictions about their future in the West. Organizations have a responsibility to destroy the myth of resettlement in a more secure part of the world. Deconstructing the myth, however, will be seen as an attempt to "de-mythologize" a fundamental necessity. Myths respond to needs: whether rational or irrational. This field research, particularly in the Sudan, demonstrated the function and the efficiency of the myth compared with the fabric of history. As noted in Chapter V, historical references prove very fragile in comparison with myths. De-mythologizing is, therefore, a very complex process. Contrary to what has been said among academics, it is quite risky to defend the idea of not giving forced migrants an opportunity to go the West. Refugees possess an idealistic representation of the "free world" and tend to consider any resettlement in the West as the best opportunity for themselves. Their vision contradicts the "disenchanted" views Western societies have of themselves. The documentary "Nomads and Pharaohs" particularly emphasises the "heavenly" image refugees have constructed of the "Far West:" a paradise so hard to reach. It is a stereotypical model of the American dream: a small house, a pretty garden and a brand new car is the universal aspiration for refugees from the Horn of Africa. The 11 September tragedy did not challenge that hope.

One of the most common conversations among refugees is that of life in Canada, America, or Australia. As one informant in Cairo puts it:

> *Every night we speak about the West. We are grown-ups now, but like teenagers we speak about our future in another world, in another reality which we consider, of course, a better world.*

The myth is absolutely durable, and this is the conclusion we can draw based on our analysis of the many voices we heard in Arba'a wa-Nus in Cairo or in Deim in Khartoum. Myths and dreams are the two escape hatches of the refugees. One informant was always "dreaming about Australia." He was going to the flea market in Cairo every day in order to buy books about Australia and was continuously "dreaming" of being resettled there. When his life was too miserable in Cairo (he could hardly afford to eat every day) he was continuously dreaming of a bright future in Australia. The essence of the dream was that dreaming was also an instrument to carry on; dreams were giving him the strength to go on and not to give up struggling. Dreams were nourishing the sense of combat. Escaping reality when it was too bad and imagining other skies was a very creative way to find internal strength.

We should not dictate to the people what they need. In this case the refugee himself found the way to keep on going. Dreams like myths are filling humans being with positive dynamics.

Imagination as theorized by Appadurai remains one strategy of exiled communities forced to move and forced to invent other norms. Societies have always proved to be much more inventive than institutions or administrations which by destiny remain "dead" bodies and disconnected from human action and achievement.

If we consider that the refugees are the "*savants de l'intérieur*" (homegrown intellectuals) we should not impose upon them our own views about the positive or negative aspects of being resettled to the West and we should not exclude them from the debate while discussing this issue.

The theoretical "bricolage" (Levi-Strauss, 1962), as stressed in the introduction, was the approach we have chosen in order to describe the reality of different African communities on the move in Cairo or in Sudan. We used different tools "(breaching", "tracking") adopted by the ethnomethodological school to investigate the field. Being a member of a community as I was (during four years of field research) gave me the essence of what it is to be a black urban nomad in a capital like Cairo.

Sharing the reality of the people I was supposed to study in an academic style gave me an outlook from below. This view is in the direct legacy of a methodology elaborated by the sociologists from the Chicago School and the "promoters" of interactionism. This valuable inheritance nevertheless implies putting the observer (or the researcher) in a risky position, as we stressed in the introduction. Interacting with vulnerable groups in exile coming from the poorest countries of this world is not a comfortable role and we discussed the existence or non-existence of an anthropology of suffering.

We pointed out in Chapter Three the cultural aspects of the Ethiopian Diaspora in transit in Cairo. We focused on the fear expressed by the Abyssinians. The extreme spatial instability (changing residence continuously) was one consequence of being illegally in Egyptian territory. Absence of rights is fabricating a new sociological profile of an urban nomad forced to move from place to place in permanent search of a shelter. Transit socio-cultural activities (the coffee ceremony for example) can be perceived as the sign of a particular vulnerability for this community. A revolution of gender is taking place in the Abyssinian community in Cairo. Ethiopian and Eritrean men in Cairo were very often escaping military obligations, on the other hand the females of the community were more or less economical migrants (the distinction remains artificial) integrated in the Cairo job market. In short, females were the breadwinners of the community and the males, most of the time, were under their material protection. Therefore it is not appropriate to consider them as a "vulnerable" group even though they are usually presented this way by the UN agencies. In Cairo, young men (deserting the army) proved to be more "vulnerable," for fear of deportation to the desert by the Egyptian police. Back in their home countries they can experience capital punishment from military tribunals.

In Chapter Four we explored the socio-cultural gap between aid agents and refugees. Aid workers were called "blond angels" by my informants in Sudan. Surprisingly they accepted to be perceived as "total saviours" interacting with "total victims." The caricature of the roles created a very simplistic relation based on dependency. Victims depended on their heroes for each spoonful of food. Refugees proved to have a deep respect and showed a total belief in everything they did "for them." "Faith" is perhaps the appropriate concept to summarize the set of perceptions that refugees express toward humanitarian staff in the camps. The concept of faith, like belief, is more related to the religious sphere. The religious dimension is one side of the problem. It is extremely unethical to put a put a human worker in an "iconic" position in front of another human (the refugee).

Camps are paradigmatic for this type of non-ethical relation (in the sense that Kant gives to the term ethic and virtue). Maintaining masses of refugees (for a long time) in a closed and controlled space produces social and economical disconnectedness. Therefore we can perceive the camp as a "total institution" (Goffman, 1968) fabricating dependency. The total institution has an impact on the subject's sense of history as seen in Chapter Five. A long exile will produce a loss of history; especially when individuals are isolated and do not rely on a group for remembering the past. In that perspective two fields of research in Cairo and Khartoum demonstrated that the sense of historicity was more fragile than the mythical discourses. In an exiled territory historical events can fade away when myths, on the contrary, are reinforced by subjectivity and imagination.

In Chapter Six we tried to index the eruption of aggression between host and aliens in an informal zone of the Egyptian capital. Filming the explosions of violence between South Sudanese refugees (Dinka) and Egyptian migrants from Upper Egypt with a digital camera in the streets of Cairo was a fruitful method to analyse the emergence of "new racisms" in the Middle-East. We experienced the expression of a new xenophobia in Egyptian society. Global stigmatization (exclusions, insults, aggressions) was a consequence of an emerging fear of invasion of Black Africans in the Arab world. In the area of Arba'a wa-Nus. Egyptians and foreigners declared that there were several thousand Sudanese refugees living on the fringe of the desert. In reality it was a question of a few hundred.

Mythical numbers (concerning the "aliens") is a shared exaggeration between refugees and hosts. Host societies in the south, as in the north (especially Europe), reveal the same kind of panic related to numbers.

Chapter Seven deepened the question of racism using the same methodology in a different neighborhood in Cairo (Dokki) with another Sudanese community from Darfur. In Dokki, we did our research in a cafeteria which was the central meeting point of the Fur community. We filmed avoidance strategies and everyday contacts between the refugees from the Fur tribe and the Egyptian host society. Small scenes reveal that social realities are in continuous construction.

Aliens and hosts cannot be apprehended with a static outlook from above. Filming gave us the opportunity to grasp the inner fluidity of social interactions between different communities. We made the effort to "zoom" in on the movements of these communities in a cultural perspective, moving with a camera in Cairo and in Sudan.

The eye of the camera tells us that *in situ* new racism arises also with new solidarities. In this concern the South Sudanese (Dinka) experience in Arba'a wa-Nus is very much comparable to the West Sudanese (Fur) experience in Dokki. In the two sites of the Egyptian capital the populations expressed contradiction and paradox related to the "feeling" of hospitality or racism. Contradictory behaviors can exist in the same spatial unit. Process of social rejection or inclusion can cohabit in the same territory.

At the end it was very stimulating to see how, at a micro-level, small scenes can override a frozen and global perception of "racism," "hospitality," "otherness." The complexity of life with a neighbor was found at this level of analysis.

In sum we have examined the human circumstances of various populations of refugees in Sudan and in Egypt, and have analyzed how their situation as refugees has made them keenly attuned to some issues, and yet somehow blind to others. In 21st-century fashion they are betwixt and between, continuously in a situation of transit.

References

Agier, M. (dir.). 1997. *Anthropologues en dangers.* Paris: Jean Michel Place.
Al-Sharmani, M. 1998. "The Somali Refugees in Cairo: Issues of Survival, Culture and Identity". Unpublished MA thesis at the American University in Cairo.
———. 2003. "Livelihood and Identity Constructions of Somali Refugees in Cairo," American University in Cairo, FMRS, Working Paper No. 2.
Amselle, J. l. 1990. *Logiques métisses.* Paris: Payot.
Anteby, L. 2004. *Les juifs éthiopiens en Israël, Les paradoxes du paradis.* Paris: CNRS Editions.
Appadurai, A. 1996. *Modernity at Large: Cultural Dimensions of Globalization.* Minneapolis: University of Minnesota Press.
———. 2000. Savoir, circulation et biographie collective, 156.2000, Intellectuels en diaspora et théories nomades <http://lhomme.revues.org/document78.html>.
Bascom, J. 1998. *Losing Place: Refugee Populations and Rural Transformations in East Africa.* New York: Berghahn Books.
Beattie, J. 1965. *Understanding an African Kingdom: Bunyoro.* New York: Holt, Rinehart, and Winston.
Bergson, H. 1939. *Matière et mémoire,* Paris, Presses Universitaires de France.
1988. *Matter and Memory.* New York: Zone Books.
Bourdieu, P. 1982. "La mort du sociologue Erving Goffman, le découvreur de l'infiniment petit," *Le Monde,* 04/12/1982.
Bourdieu, P. 1993. *La misère du Monde.* Paris: Seuil.
Brown, N., S. Riordan, and M. Sharpe. 2003. "Plus ça change, plus c'est la même chose: The Insecurity of Eritreans and Ethiopians in Cairo." A FMRS report, Cairo, American University in Cairo.
Burgess, E. 1925. "The Growth of the City: An Introduction to a Research Project." In R. Park, E. Burgess, and R.D. Mc Kenzie, *The City.* Chicago: University of Chicago Press.

Charney, D.S., E.J. Nestler, and B.S. Bunney, eds. 1999. *Neurobiology of Mental Illness*. New York: Oxford University Press.

Cooper, D. 1992. *Urban Refugees: Ethiopians and Eritreans in Cairo, Cairo Papers in Social Science* 15(2), Summer.

Curley, B. 2002. "Aragi: An Ethnography of Sudanese Displacement." Unpublished MA Thesis, American University in Cairo.

Davis, J. 1992. "The Anthropology of Suffering," *Journal of Refugee Studies* 5(2):149–161.

De Certeau, M. 1975. *L'écriture de l'histoire*. Paris: Gallimard.

De Montclos, Marc Antoine Pérouse. 2001. *Migrations forcées et urbanisation*. Paris: Ceped.

Devereux, G. 1967. *From Anxiety to Method in the Behavioral Sciences*. The Hague: Mouton.

Direche-Slimani, K. and F. Le Houérou. 2002. *Les Comoriens à Marseille: d'une mémoire à l'autre*. Paris: Editions Autrement.

Duman, R.S. and D.S. Charney. 1999. "Cell Atrophy and Loss in Major Depression," *Biological Psychiatry* 45 (9):1083-1084.

El Kadi, G. 1987. *L'urbanisation spontanée au Caire*. Tours: Orstom/Urbama.

Evans-Pritchard, E.E. 1969. *The Nuer: A Description of the Modes of Livelihood and Political Institutions of a Nilotic People*. Oxford: Clarendon Press.

Fabos, A.1999. "Ambiguous Ethnicity: Propriety (Adab) as a Situational Boundary Marker for Northern Sudanese in Cairo." Unpublished PhD thesis, Boston University.

Fawzy-Rossano, D. 2002. *Le Soudan en question*. Paris: La Table Ronde.

Freidson, E. 1983. "Celebrating Erving Goffman," *Contemporary Sociology* 12(4):359–362, July.

Fukuyama, F. 1992. *The End of History and the Last Man*. New York: Free Press.

1992. *La fin de l'histoire et le dernier homme*. Paris: Flammarion.

Garfinkel, H. 1967. *Studies in Ethnomethodology*. Englehood Cliffs, NJ: Prentice Hall.

———. 1986. *Ethnomethodological Studies of Work*. London: Routledge & Kegan Paul.

———. 2002. *Ethnomethodology's Program*. New York: Rowan and Littlefield.

Gell, A. 1992. *The Anthropology of Time: Cultural Constructions of Temporal Maps*. Oxford: Berg Publishers.

Goffman, E. 1959. *The Presentation of Self in Everyday Life*. New York: Doubleday Anchor.

———. 1963. *Stigma: Notes on the Management of Spoiled Identity*. Englewood Cliffs, NJ: Prentice-Hall.

———. 1968. *Asylums: Essays on the Social Situation of Mental Patients and Other Inmates*. Harmondsworth: Penguin Books.

1968. *Asile*. Paris: Editions de Minuit.
1973. *La mise en scène du quotidien*. Paris: Editions de Minuit.
1975. *Stigmate, Les usages sociaux des handicaps*. Paris: Editions de Minuit.
Halbwachs, M. 1994. *Les cadres sociaux de la mémoire*. Paris: Albin Michel.
———. 1997. *La mémoire collective*. Paris: Albin Michel.
Harrell-Bond, B. 1986. *Imposing Aid*. Oxford: Oxford University Press.
———. 2002. "Can Humanitarian Work with Refugees be Humane?", *Human Rights Quarterly* 24:51–85.
Hopkins, N., S. Mehanna, and S. El Haggar. 2001. *People and Pollution*. Cairo: The American University in Cairo Press.
Ibn el Tounsy, Mohammed Omar. 1851. *Voyage au Ouaday*. Paris: Perron Editeur.
Isotalo, R. 2001. "Palestinian Return Migration: Questions of Dispersion, Cohesion, and Hierarchy. Paper presented at Palestinian Return Migration: Socio-economic and Cultural Approaches organized by MEAWARDS (Population Council) and Palestinanian Refugee and Diaspora Center Shaml, Ramallah, June 13–14, 2001.
Kant, E. The Critique of Judgement. Oxford: Oxford University Press.
1984. *Critique de la faculté de juger*. Paris: Vrin, Bibliothèque des textes philosophiques.
Karadawi, A. 1999. *Refugee Policy in Sudan: 1967–1984*. New York: Berghahn.
Kibreab, G. 1996. "Eritrean and Ethiopian Urban Refugees in Khartoum: What the Eye Refuses to See," *African Studies Review* 39(3):131–178.
Kuhlman, T. 1990. *Burden or Boon? A study of Eritrean Refugees in the Sudan*. Amsterdam: VU University Press.
———. 1994. *Asylum or Aid? The Economic Integration of Ethiopian and Eritrean Refugees in the Sudan*. Aldershot: Avebury for African Studies Centre.
Le Goff, J. 1992. *History and Memory*. New York: Columbia University Press.
1998. *Histoire et mémoire*. Paris: Gallimard.
Le Houérou, F. 2000. *Ethiopie-Erythrée: frères ennemis de la corne de l'Afrique* Paris: L'Harmattan.
———. 2003. "Les camps de la soif au Soudan," *Le Monde Diplomatique*, Mai 2003, p.26.
———. 2004. *Migrants forcés éthiopiens et érythréens en Egypte et au Soudan, passagers d'un monde à l'autre*. Paris: L'Harmattan.
Leinhardt, G. 1961. *Divinity and Experience: The Religion of the Dinka*. Oxford: Oxford University Press.
Levi-Strauss, C. 1962. *La pensée sauvage*. Paris: Plon.
1966. *The Savage Mind*. Chicago: University of Chicago Press.
MacMichael, H.A. 1967. *A History of the Arabs in the Sudan, and Some Account of the People Who Preceded Them and of the Tribes Inhabiting Darfur*. London: Cass.

Malkki, L. 1987. *Purity and Exile: Violence, Memory and National Cosmology among Hutu Refugees in Tanzania*. Chicago: The University of Chicago Press.

Nadel, S.F. 1945. "Notes on Bani Amer Society, Khartoum," *Sudan Notes and Records*, vol. XXVI, part 1.

Markakis, J. 1987. *National and Class Conflict in the Horn of Africa*. Cambridge: Cambridge University Press.

Nordstrom, C. and A. Robben, eds. 1984. *Fieldwork under Fire: Contemporary Studies of Violence and Survival*. Los Angeles: University of California Press.

Park, R, E. Burgess, and R.D. Mc Kenzie. 1925. *The City*. Chicago: University of Chicago Press.

Pollera, A. 1935. *Le popolazioni indigene dell'Eritrea*. Bologna: Licino Cappelli, Rocca S. Casciano.

Prunier, G. 2002. "Sudan: irreconcilable differences," *Le Monde Diplomatique*, English language edition, December <http://www.monde-diplomatique.fr/2002/12/PRUNIER/ 17270>.

Raulin, A. 2000. *L'ethnique est quotidien, Diasporas, marchés et cultures métropolitaines*. Paris: L'Harmattan.

Razzaz, O. 1993. "Urban Settlement Around Amman," *Middle East Report*, March-April.

Robben, A.C.G.M. 1984. "The Politics of Truth and Emotion among Victims and Perpetrators of Violence." In C. Nordstrom and A. Robben., eds., *Fieldwork under Fire: Contemporary Studies of Violence and Survival*. Los Angeles: University of California Press, pp. 81–103.

Signoles, P., G. El Kadi, and R. Sidi Boumedine (dir). 1999. *L'urbain dans le monde arabe: politiques, instruments et acteurs*. Paris: CNRS éditions.

Thomas, N. 1989. *Out of Time*. Cambridge: Cambridge University Press.

Walkup, M. 1997. "Policy dysfunction in humanitarian organizations: the role of coping strategies, institutions and organizational culture," *Journal of Refugee Studies* 10(1):37–60.

Walz, T. 1978. *Trade between Egypt and Bilad As-Sudan: 1700–1820*. Cairo: Institut Français d'Archéologie Orientale.

Wieviorka, M. 2001. *La différence*. Paris: Balland.

Zohry, A. 2002. "Unskilled Temporary Labour Migration from Upper Egypt to Cairo." Unpublished conference paper, CEDEJ.

About the Author

DR. FABIENNE LE HOUÉROU is a researcher at the Centre National de la Recherche Scientifique (CNRS). A historian specialized in the Horn of Africa, she published a number of books on Ethiopia and Eritrea, including *L'épopée des soldats de Mussolini en Abyssinie 1936–1938: les ensablés* and *Ethiopie-Erythree: frères ennemis de la Corne de l'Afrique*. Combining film with ethnography, she directed "Nomads and Pharaohs", a documentary produced by TV5, Citizen Television, KTO and the CNRS Images.

CAIRO PAPERS IN SOCIAL SCIENCE

Volume One 1977–1978
1 *Women, Health and Development, Cynthia Nelson, ed.
2 *Democracy in Egypt, Ali E. Hillal Dessouki, ed.
3 *Mass Communications and the October War, Olfat Hassan Agha
4 *Rural Resettlement in Egypt, Helmy Tadros
5 *Saudi Arabian Bedouin, Saad E. Ibrahim and Donald P. Cole

Volume Two 1978–1979
1 *Coping With Poverty in a Cairo Community, Andrea B. Rugh
2 *Modernization of Labor in the Arab Gulf, Enid Hill
3 Studies in Egyptian Political Economy, Herbert M. Thompson
4 *Law and Social Change in Contemporary Egypt, Cynthia Nelson and Klaus Friedrich Koch, eds.
5 *The Brain Drain in Egypt, Saneya Saleh

Volume Three 1979–1980
1 *Party and Peasant in Syria, Raymond Hinnebusch
2 *Child Development in Egypt, Nicholas V. Ciaccio
3 *Living Without Water, Asaad Nadim et. al.
4 *Export of Egyptian School Teachers, Suzanne A. Messiha
5 *Population and Urbanization in Morocco, Saad E. Ibrahim

Volume Four 1980–1981
1 *Cairo's Nubian Families, Peter Geiser
2, 3 *Symposium on Social Research for Development: Proceedings, Social Research Center
4 *Women and Work in the Arab World, Earl L. Sullivan and Karima Korayem

Volume Five 1982
1 *Ghagar of Sett Guiranha: A Study of a Gypsy Community in Egypt, Nabil Sobhi Hanna
2 *Distribution of Disposal Income and the Impact of Eliminating Food Subsidies in Egypt, Karima Korayem
3 *Income Distribution and Basic Needs in Urban Egypt, Amr Mohie el-Din

Volume Six 1983
1 *The Political Economy of Revolutionary Iran, Mihssen Kadhim

2   *Urban Research Strategies in Egypt, Richard A. Lobban, ed.
3   *Non-alignment in a Changing World, Mohammed el-Sayed Selim, ed.
4   *The Nationalization of Arabic and Islamic Education in Egypt: Dar al-Alum and al-Azhar, Lois A. Arioan

Volume Seven 1984
1   *Social Security and the Family in Egypt, Helmi Tadros
2   *Basic Needs, Inflation and the Poor of Egypt, Myrette el-Sokkary
3   *The Impact of Development Assistance On Egypt, Earl L. Sullivan, ed.
4   *Irrigation and Society in Rural Egypt, Sohair Mehanna, Richard Huntington and Rachad Antonius

Volume Eight 1985
1, 2   *Analytic Index of Survey Research in Egypt, Madiha el-Safty, Monte Palmer and Mark Kennedy

Volume Nine 1986
1   *Philosophy, Ethics and Virtuous Rule, Charles E. Butterworth
2   The 'Jihad': An Islamic Alternative in Egypt, Nemat Guenena
3   *The Institutionalization of Palestinian Identity in Egypt, Maha A. Dajani
4   *Social Identity and Class in a Cairo Neighborhood, Nadia A. Taher

Volume Ten 1987
1   *Al-Sanhuri and Islamic Law, Enid Hill
2   *Gone For Good, Ralph Sell
3   *The Changing Image of Women in Rural Egypt, Mona Abaza
4   *Informal Communities in Cairo: the Basis of a Typology, Linda Oldham, Haguer el Hadidi, Hussein Tamaa

Volume Eleven 1988
1   *Participation and Community in Egyptian New Lands: the Case of South Tahrir, Nicholas Hopkins et. al.
2   Palestinian Universities Under Occupation, Antony T. Sullivan
3   Legislating Infitah: Investment, Foreign Trade and Currency Laws, Khaled M. Fahmy
4   Social History of An Agrarian Reform Community in Egypt, Reem Saad

Volume Twelve 1989
1   *Cairo's Leap Forward: People, Households and Dwelling Space, Fredric Shorter
2   *Women, Water and Sanitation: Household Water Use in Two Egyptian Villages, Samiha el-Katsha et. al.

3   *Palestinian Labor in a Dependent Economy: Women Workers in the West Bank Clothing Industry*, Randa Siniora
4   *The Oil Question in Egyptian-Israeli Relations, 1967–1979: A Study in International Law and Resource Politics*, Karim Wissa

Volume Thirteen 1990
1   **Squatter Markets in Cairo*, Helmi R. Tadros, Mohamed Feteeha, Allen Hibbard
2   **The Sub-culture of Hashish Users in Egypt: A Descriptive Analytic Study*, Nashaat Hassan Hussein
3   **Social Background and Bureaucratic Behavior in Egypt*, Earl L. Sullivan, el Sayed Yassin, Ali Leila, Monte Palmer
4   **Privatization: the Egyptian Debate*, Mostafa Kamel el-Sayyid

Volume Fourteen 1991
1   **Perspectives on the Gulf Crisis*, Dan Tschirgi and Bassam Tibi
2   **Experience and Expression: Life Among Bedouin Women in South Sinai*, Deborah Wickering
3   *Impact of Temporary International Migration on Rural Egypt*, Atef Hanna Nada
4   **Informal Sector in Egypt*, Nicholas S. Hopkins ed.

Volume Fifteen, 1992
1   **Scenes of Schooling: Inside a Girls' School in Cairo*, Linda Herrera
2   *Urban Refugees: Ethiopians and Eritreans in Cairo*, Dereck Cooper
3   *Investors and Workers in the Western Desert of Egypt: An Exploratory Survey*, Naeim Sherbiny, Donald Cole, Nadia Makary
4   **Environmental Challenges in Egypt and the World*, Nicholas S. Hopkins, ed.

Volume Sixteen, 1993
1   **The Socialist Labor Party: A Case Study of a Contemporary Egyptian Opposition Party*, Hanaa Fikry Singer
2   **The Empowerment of Women: Water and Sanitation Iniatives in Rural Egypt*, Samiha el Katsha, Susan Watts
3   *The Economics and Politics of Structural Adjustment in Egypt: Third Annual Symposium*
4   **Experiments in Community Development in a Zabbaleen Settlement*, Marie Assaad and Nadra Garas

Volume Seventeen, 1994
1   *Democratization in Rural Egypt: a Study of the Village Local Popular Council*, Hanan Hamdy Radwan

2   *Farmers and Merchants: Background for Structural Adjustment in Egypt*, Sohair Mehanna, Nicholas S. Hopkins and Bahgat Abdelmaksoud
3   *Human Rights: Egypt and the Arab World, Fourth Annual Symposium*
4   *Environmental Threats in Egypt: Perceptions and Actions*, Salwa S. Gomaa, ed.

Volume Eighteen, 1995
1   *Social Policy in the Arab World*, Jacqueline Ismael & Tareq Y. Ismael
2   *Workers, Trade Union and the State in Egypt: 1984-1989*, Omar el-Shafie
3   *The Development of Social Science in Egypt: Economics, History and Sociology; Fifth Annual Symposium*
4   *Structural Adjustment, Stabilization Policies and the Poor in Egypt*, Karima Korayem

Volume Nineteen, 1996
1   *Nilopolitics: A Hydrological Regime, 1870–1990*, Mohamed Hatem el-Atawy
2   **Images of the Other: Europe and the Muslim World Before 1700*, David R. Blanks et al.
3   **Grass Roots Participation in the Development of Egypt*, Saad Eddin Ibrahim et al.
4   The *Zabbalin Community of Muqattam*, Elena Volpi and Doaa Abdel Motaal

Volume Twenty, 1997
1   *Class, Family and Power in an Egyptian Village*, Samer el-Karanshawy
2   *The Middle East and Development in a Changing World*, Donald Heisel, ed.
3   *Arab Regional Women's Studies Workshop*, Cynthia Nelson and Soraya Altorki, eds.
    "Just a Gaze": Female Clientele of Diet Clinics in Cairo: an Ethnomedical Study, Iman Farid Bassyouny

Volume Twenty-one, 1998
1   *Turkish Foreign Policy During the Gulf War of 1990–1991*, Mostafa Aydin
2   *State and Industrial Capitalism in Egypt*, Samer Soliman
3   *Twenty Years of Development in Egypt (1977–1997): Part I*, Mark C. Kennedy
4   *Twenty Years of Development in Egypt (1977–1997): Part II*, Mark C. Kennedy

Volume Twenty-two, 1999
1   *Poverty and Poverty Alleviation Strategies in Egypt*, Ragui Assaad and Malak Rouchdy
2   *Between Field and Text: Emerging Voices in Egyptian Social Science*, Seteney Shami and Linda Hererra, eds.
3   *Masters of the Trade: Crafts and Craftspeople in Cairo, 1750–1850*, Pascale Ghazaleh
4   *Discourses in Contemporary Egypt: Politics and Social Issues*, Enid Hill, ed.

Volume Twenty-three, 2000

1. *Fiscal Policy Measures in Egypt: Public Debt and Food Subsidy,* Gouda Abdel-Khalek and Karima Korayem
2. *New Frontiers in the Social History of the Middle East,* Enid Hill, ed.
3. *Egyptian Encounters,* Jason Thompson, ed.
4. *Women's Perception of Environmental Change in Egypt,* Eman el Ramly

Volume Twenty-four, 2001

1, 2. *The New Arab Family,* Nicholas S. Hopkins, ed.
3. *An Investigation of the Phenomenon of Polygyny in Rural Egypt,* Laila S. Shahd
4. *The Terms of Empowerment: Islamic Women Activists in Egypt,* Sherine Hafez

Volume Twenty-five, 2002

1, 2. *Elections in the Middle East: What do they Mean?* Iman A. Hamdy, ed.
3. *Employment Crisis of Female Graduates in Egypt: An Ethnographic Account,* Ghada F. Barsoum
4. *Palestinian and Israeli Nationalism: Identity Politics and Education in Jerusalem,* Evan S. Weiss

Volume Twenty-six, 2003

1. *Culture and Natural Environment: Ancient and Modern Middle Eastern Texts,* Sharif S. Elmusa, ed.
2. *Street Children in Egypt: Group Dynamics and Subcultural Constituents,* Nashaat Hussein
3. *IMF–Egyptian Debt Negotiations,* Bessma Momani
4. *Forced Migrants and Host Societies in Egypt and Sudan,* Fabienne Le Houérou

* currently out of print

لقد أرادت الباحثة من خلال تعرضها لجماعات مختلفة من الهجرة القسرية سواء فى المدن أو المخيمات أن تعطى صورة حية لتجربة تلك الجماعات بهدف التركيز على مصيرها المشترك فى العالم العربى والقاء الضوء على ظاهرة الهجرة من الجنوب الى الجنوب التى تعد مثالاً على العولمة من أسفل.

ملخص

تعد منطقة القرن الافريقى من اكثر مناطق العالم فقراً حيث يجتاحها الجفاف والمجاعات والحروب الأهلية، مما دفع قطاع كبير من سكانها الى الهجرة القسرية الى دول الغرب. ونظراً للقرب الجغرافى فإن المحطة الأولى فى هذه الرحلة هى السودان تليها مصر.

يقوم هذا البحث على دراسة ميدانية للهجرة المؤقتة من اثيوبيا واريتريا والسودان الى كل من مصر والسودان خلال الفترة من عام ٢٠٠٠ الى ٢٠٠٤ بغرض التعرف على رؤية المهاجرين لهويتهم وأوضاعهم وعلاقتهم بالمجتمعات المضيفة ومنظمات الاغاثة الانسانية.

تنقسم الدراسة الى ثمانية فصول تبدأ بالفصل الأول وهو المقدمة. فى الفصل الثانى يتم تقديم الاطار النظرى للبحث يليه عرض لأهم الجوانب الثقافية والاجتماعية للهجرة الاثيوبية المؤقتة فى القاهرة فى الفصل الثالث. أما الفصل الرابع فيشرح العلاقة بين اللاجئين وموظفى الاغاثة الانسانية فى صحراء السودان من خلال التركيز على تجربة اللاجئين الارتريين فى منطقة كسالا التى تقع فى الشمال الشرقى من السودان. ويتناول الفصل الخامس تجربة أخرى للاجئين فى السودان – هم لاجئو اثيوبيا الذين يقطنون فى حى الديم فى الخرطوم – حيث يحاول اكتشاف العلاقة المتداخلة بين المنفى والذاكرة والتاريخ فى تشكيل وعى هؤلاء اللاجئين. ومن الخرطوم الى القاهرة، ينقل الفصل السادس تجربة لاجئى دنكة جنوب السودان فى عزبة أربعه ونص – وهو أحد الأحياء العشوائية الفقيرة يقع على بعد أربع كيلومترات ونصف على طريق القاهرة – السويس – وعلاقتهم اليومية بسكان المنطقة من المصريين. وأخيراً، يقدم الفصل السابع العلاقة بين اللاجئين السودانيين من دارفور و المصريين من خلال دراسة حالة لتجربة عائشة – اللاجئة السودانية التى تدير كافيتريا فى حى الدقى، بينما تأتى خاتمة البحث فى الفصل الثامن.

حقوق النشر محفوظة لقسم النشر بالجامعة الامريكية بالقاهرة
١١٣ شارع قصر العيني، القاهرة – مصر
طبعة أولى: ٢٠٠٦
جميع الحقوق محفوظة. ممنوع اعادة طبع أى جزء من الكتاب أو حفظه بعد تصحيحه أو نقله فى أية صورة أو بأية واسطة الكترونية أو ميكانيكية أو تصويرية أو تسجيلية أو غير ذلك بدون التصريح المسبق من صاحب حق النشر.

رقم دار الكتب: ٠٥/١١٣٦٩
الترقيم الدولى: X ٩٦٤ ٤٢٤ ٩٧٧

بحوث القاهرة في العلوم الاجتماعية

مجلد ٢٦   عدد ٤   شتاء ٢٠٠٣

الهجرة القسرية والمجتمعات المضيفة في مصر والسودان

فابيان لأورو

قسم النشر بالجامعة الامريكية بالقاهرة